"I can't believe I'm really doing this," I mumbled to myself as we entered the theater.

Abby looked at me strangely. "What do you mean, Joy? What are you doing?"

I coughed. "Uh, seeing the ballet in New York, of course. It's a dream come true."

She smiled. "Well, calm down. You're a bundle of nerves. Anyone would think it was you who's performing tonight instead of Alissa."

My stomach did a somersault. It was a good thing Abby wasn't looking back at the wide eyes of the Forever Friends behind her. Their surprised looks would have given me away for sure.

That's What Friends Are For!

Cindy Savage

Cover illustration by Richard Kriegler

To Natalie—
thanks for being my friend

Published by Willowisp Press, Inc.
401 E. Wilson Bridge Road, Worthington, Ohio 43085

Printed in the United States of America
10 9 8 7 6 5 4 3 2 1

ISBN 0-87406-407-4

One

I plopped down on the sofa in our living room for our daily Forever Friends Club meeting. I just love our meetings. They are so much fun. We all get along so well, and we talk about everything. Of course, we do have to spend some time talking about Party Time, our business. But today, Krissy Branch, one of the members of our club, was late coming home from school. So, Aimee Lawrence, Linda Jean Jacobs, and I, Joy Marshall, were just sitting around talking.

"Are you ready for vacation?" I asked Linda Jean. "It's only a few days away."

"Are you kidding? I've been ready since September," she answered.

I laughed. Linda Jean gets really good grades. But she would rather be taking care of her backyard zoo than studying.

"How about you, Joy?" Krissy asked. "I suppose if it were up to you, we'd go to school all year long."

"Well...," I hedged and then laughed.

Aimee threw a pillow at me. She ducked as I threw it back and reached for a finger sandwich on a plate sitting on the coffee table.

"Okay. I admit it. Even I am looking forward to the two-week break. It will give me the chance to practice a few new dance steps and work out routines for our January parties."

"Don't you ever slow down and relax?" Linda Jean teased.

I was about to launch another pillow attack when Krissy burst through the door into our living room.

"I'm here!" she announced, tossing her long blond hair behind her shoulder.

"How was marching band practice?" Aimee asked her, picking up the papers that had been blown off the table by Hurricane Kristina.

"It was fine, but hectic," she said. Krissy grinned and sat down on the chair. "I stopped by my house on the way here," she explained. "And I picked up my mail."

"And?" We all leaned forward to hear what

news she had to tell us.

"You're not going to believe this," she said. "I got a letter from Alissa O'Toole."

"Do you mean Alissa O'Toole, the famous actress you met when your family went to Los Angeles last summer?" I asked.

"That's the one," Krissy said. "Remember I told you that Alissa is the same age as us?"

"But she has already been in lots of movies and television shows," I finished for her. "So, what did she have to say? Is there another movie role tryout for your sister, Kitty?"

"It's better than that!" Krissy waved the letter around, trying to draw out the suspense. Finally, just when we couldn't stand waiting another minute, Aimee snatched the piece of paper out of Krissy's hand. Aimee pulled the letter from the envelope and read it aloud.

Dear Krissy,

I'm not sure if you'll remember me, but I met you in the studio commissary when you and your sister were eating lunch there last July. Remember I said that I wished you lived near me because I would like Party Time to give a party for me? Well, I'm turning 12 on December 30, and my mother says I can have

Party Time give my party. What do you think?

"How are we supposed to give a party for Alissa O'Toole in Los Angeles when we live in Atlanta?" Linda Jean asked. "Is she coming here for a role she's playing?"

Krissy shook her head, while Aimee read on, wide-eyed and excited.

My regular home is in New York. I want to fly all of you up here to spend the week between Christmas and New Year's. We can go shopping and to the theater, and whatever else you want. Please say yes. I'll pay for everything. Just say you'll come.

Love,
Alissa .

"Wow, New York!" I shouted. "That would be great! We could go to the ballet!"

"And we could go to the art museums," said Aimee.

"How about the Bronx Zoo?" asked Linda Jean.

"Boy, I've always wanted to go to New York," Krissy said. "I want to see where King Kong climbed the Empire State Building."

"Hey, wait a minute," I said. "I hate to dampen everyone's excitement, but we have something to think about before we get too carried away. What if our parents won't let us go to New York?"

"Why wouldn't they let us go? We don't have to pay for anything," Krissy said.

"Oh, they might object to little things like the fact that New York is over 1,000 miles away from Atlanta, and that we would have to fly on an airplane in winter and stay alone in a strange city. You know how parents panic over stuff like that," I informed her.

"Will we have to stay in a hotel?" Linda Jean asked.

"No, we won't," Aimee said, holding up Alissa's letter. "Alissa says that we can stay at her house. She says she lives someplace called the Hamptons, and that they have plenty of room for all of us."

"She lives in the Hamptons?" I exclaimed. "That's where my cousin Patty moved to from Rock Creek, Arkansas last month. I haven't seen her in a year. You all remember Patty, don't you? It sure would be neat to see her again."

"She must have a huge house," Linda Jean said, changing the subject back to Alissa. "Alissa O'Toole must be really rich if she can afford to fly us all up to New York for a week and take us sightseeing. She probably has maids and servants and cooks and everything! I wonder why she wants Party Time to do her party. There must be tons of other entertainment businesses in New York."

"Quit trying to give this job away to someone else," Krissy said, punching Linda Jean lightly on the arm. "Alissa O'Toole wants Party Time and the Forever Friends because we're the best."

"It's certainly not because we're the most modest," Aimee joked.

"Let's go tell Abby," I said. "We'll see what she thinks."

Abby is my mom. I'm not sure why I call her by her first name, but it feels right. Maybe it's because Aimee and Krissy have always called her Abby since we were babies together. And ever since Linda Jean moved to Atlanta a couple of years ago, she's called my mom Abby. It just seems natural for me to call her Abby, too. She seems more like a friend to me than a mom. After all, we are in business together.

Abby's Catering and Party Time work together to give the best, the tastiest, and the most fun-filled parties around. We've even been interviewed on a TV talk show.

We all trooped into the kitchen with our hands behind our backs. We stood still for a minute while we waited for Abby to notice us.

"So, you finally decided to come help with the parmesan crisps?" Abby asked, not turning around from the marble countertop where she was rolling dough.

"Actually, we came to talk," I said seriously.

"Work while you talk," she said. "I have to deliver these hors d'oeuvres centerpiece baskets to The Grange by seven o'clock."

We put on our aprons and hair nets. We washed our hands with hot water and disinfectant soap.

"What do you want us to do?" Linda Jean asked.

"You tie the sesame crackers into bundles," she told Linda Jean. "Aimee, you sprinkle parmesan cheese on the breadsticks and twist them before they go into the oven. Joy, why don't you and Krissy begin lining the baskets with those checkered napkins?"

Taking our places quickly around the

kitchen counter, we began our assigned tasks. The Forever Friends were used to helping out. We helped Abby with her catering chores almost every day.

"What do you want to talk about?" Abby asked as she pulled another tray of parmesan sticks out of the oven and set them on a cooling rack.

"We want to talk to you about going to New York," I said casually. "We thought we'd take a trip up there around the holidays. What do you think?"

"Well, that definitely sounds like fun," she said, playing along. "I hope you have some warm clothes to take. I hear it's pretty cold up there this time of year."

"We'll just pick up some coats at Bloomingdale's," added Aimee. "I hear they have great sales there after Christmas."

"I'm sure they do," Abby said. She couldn't hold back her laugh. She turned around and faced us. "Okay, so what's this New York stuff all about?"

I started to make another joke, but I couldn't keep the news from her any longer.

"Alissa O'Toole has asked Party Time to do a party for her in New York!" I told Abby excitedly. "It's for her birthday on December 30. She says she'll pay for everything. Can we go, Abby? Please?"

"Who is Alissa O'Toole?" Abby asked.

Aimee handed the letter to Abby, and we all held our breaths while she read it slowly and carefully.

"I know you won't like to hear this," she said after she'd finished reading the letter. "But I think all of you are a bit young to take this kind of trip by yourselves."

"Abby," I said. "We're old enough to run our own business and to help out with yours."

"We're old enough to ride our bikes all over the place to make deliveries for you," Aimee said in defense.

"Yes, but New York is a much bigger city than Atlanta. There is so much crime there."

"We won't be around criminals," Linda Jean told her. "Alissa said she'd personally take us shopping and stuff. I'm sure there will be plenty of chaperons. And she sounds as if she really wants us to come."

"Well..." Abby said, shaking her head.

"Liza went to California for two whole weeks when she was 13 years old," I said, reminding her of my sister's trip to Hollywood when she won a local radio contest.

"That was different. Your dad went with her," Abby added.

"Well, I'm sure he wasn't with her every minute," I continued. "Besides, I'm sure Mrs. O'Toole will be with us some of the time. And wouldn't it be great if I could see Patty, too, while I was there?"

We wrapped and packaged the food as we talked more about New York. We just had to convince Abby that we should do this party for Alissa.

"Why don't all of you go home and discuss this trip with your parents?" Abby suggested. "I can't make the decision for them. But I do think we need more information from Alissa's mother before we can make a final decision. Then we can get our four families together for a conference to okay the arrangements."

"Okay the arrangements?" I asked. "Does that mean we can go?"

Abby smiled. "It means I'm thinking about it."

Two

WITHIN an hour we had finished packing 27 baskets with tasty hors d'oeuvres of all kinds.

"The baskets are really pretty. I just love the red bows and the sprigs of greenery," Aimee said. "They look so festive." Since Aimee is the artist in our group, we always put her in charge of the decorations.

"In just a few hours, only the napkins will be left in these baskets," I said. "But I guess that means we've done our job well."

We all stood around looking at our handiwork. Parmesan cheese-covered breadsticks twisted out of one end of each basket. Foil-covered packages of shrimp puffs were nestled next to stuffed olives and meatballs on decorated toothpicks. My favorite hors d'oeuvre was the miniature tortilla rolled around a mixture of chopped chicken, green pepper strips, and cheese. Mmmm.

"Why don't you take a picture of the baskets?" my dad suggested as he came through the front door.

"Hi, Dad," I said, giving him a big hug. It was Friday night, and he was home from work. He trains supermarket managers all over Georgia and north Florida. I couldn't wait to tell him about the trip to New York.

Abby snapped a couple of instant pictures and slid the finished prints into our special memories album. Inside the album, we displayed pictures of the Forever Friends Club. There were even pictures of Aimee, Krissy, and me as babies. Since Linda Jean only moved to Atlanta a couple of years ago, there are no pictures of her as a baby in the album.

There were pictures of the Forever Friends Club doing odd jobs for Abby as we grew up. And, of course, there were pictures of us giving our Party Time parties and helping with Abby's catering events. Abby put the pictures of the baskets next to the only picture we had of Shannon Kellar's unicorn fantasy cake before her dog put his big paws into it.

"Welcome home," Abby said to John, my dad. "The girls have some big news to tell you."

"We've been offered an all-expenses-paid trip to New York!" I announced to my dad.

"I can't wait to hear about this one," he said, grinning.

They went into the kitchen as I said good-bye to my friends at the door.

"Good luck convincing your parents about the New York trip. Call me, and tell me what they say," I said to Krissy, Aimee, and Linda Jean.

"Yeah," said Aimee. "I'm so excited. I know I won't be able to wait until tomorrow morning to find out if we can go or not." She skipped down the front steps, humming one of the tunes from *A Chorus Line.*

Her humming reminded me of my favorite tune—the theme from the *Nutcracker.* I closed the front door and did a pirouette and ballet leaps down the hall toward the kitchen.

I was halfway down the hall when the doorbell rang. I leaped back to answer it. I figured that Krissy or Aimee forgot something. But when I opened the door, there stood Liza and my nephew, Jeremiah. He held his baby arms out to me and said, "Awk, na na, ba."

"That means, 'Hi, Aunt Joy. I can walk,'" Liza explained.

"You can walk? What a big boy you are, Jeremiah," I said, taking him out of Liza's arms and placing him on his feet in the hallway.

I let go of him gently. Jeremiah stood there solidly, with his feet spread apart and a silly grin on his face.

"Come to Auntie Joy," I said to him. "Walk to me, Jeremiah."

He took one step, two steps, and then he fell on his padded bottom.

I scooped him up and headed for the kitchen. "That was great, Jeremiah. Let's go show Grandma what you can do."

Liza followed behind me lugging Jeremiah's diaper bag and her purse.

"What's new?" she asked me.

"Oh, nothing much. I may be going to New York for a week. That's all."

I didn't give her a chance to ask any questions. I savored the look on her face. It was a mixture of disbelief and envy. I made myself busy showing Abby and John how terrific Jeremiah was at walking. He was only 10 months old, so I thought his taking two steps was pretty good.

My parents thought so, too. I could tell from the silly grins on their faces. They invited Liza to stay for dinner and set up Jeremiah's special high chair that we have for when he visits.

"Thanks," Liza said, accepting their invitation. "I've been gift shopping all afternoon, and I didn't feel like going home to an empty apartment to fix dinner."

"Where's Mike?" Abby asked. Mike is Liza's husband, and they're almost always together.

"He had to work late on a computer program at the office. The boss wants it tomorrow, and he's paying Mike double time to stay late to finish it. The extra money will definitely come in handy."

"Did you get your new drapes up in the bedroom?" Abby asked.

Liza launched into a long story about the trouble with ready-made curtains and how they never really fit properly. I let my mind wander to the snow-covered streets of New York City.

Would we see the Statue of Liberty? Would we be able to stay for the dropping of the ball in Times Square on New Year's Eve? Would we be able to go to the ballet? Would we be able to give a terrific enough party to satisfy a rich and famous movie star?

I admit I was just a little nervous about the whole thing. I decided to write a letter to my cousin Patty right after dinner. Since she lives in New York, I was hoping that I'd be able to see her while we were there—if we even got to go.

"Tell me about your trip to New York," Liza said, breaking into my thoughts.

I told her the whole story from beginning to end, from Krissy's meeting Alissa O'Toole in California to the letter Krissy had just received inviting Party Time to do Alissa's birthday party.

"I really want to go. I think this would be a terrific opportunity for me," I said, trying to sound responsible and mature.

"I don't know," Abby said again. "You girls could get into a lot of trouble in New York—especially if you don't have the proper supervision. I don't know how much time Mrs. O'Toole is willing to give up to supervise you."

Liza swallowed her mouthful of food with a gulp. "I'd let them go," she said, surprising me. Liza is usually much more protective of me than Abby is. She has never stopped treating me like a baby. Maybe now that she has Jeremiah, I'm starting to look more grown up in comparison. I sat up straight as I listened for what Abby and John would say.

"Why do you think they should be allowed to go, Liza?" John prompted.

"Well, for one thing, Joy is very responsible. I trust her to look after Jeremiah, and that's a lot of responsibility. She and the Forever Friends are responsible for handling groups of little kids for hours at a time. Going to New York would be a great learning experience for Joy. And they'd be staying with the O'Tooles. It's not like they'd be in a hotel by themselves," Liza finished.

"Thanks, Liza," I said, smiling.

John and Abby were thoughtful. "Facts," John finally said. "You need more facts about the trip, Joy. I want to know all the details about this trip. I want to know who you are going to be with, who is going to be chaperon, how late you are going to stay up—that kind of thing. And I would feel much more comfortable if Abby or one of the other parents went along with you. I'd love to go, but I have to be out of town again."

I giggled. "You sound like my English

teacher. When we're doing a report, she always tells us to think of the facts. Then she tells us to back up our facts with examples and more details."

"It's called planning. I have to plan ahead for the weeks that I go out of town. That way, if there is an emergency, any one of you can reach me."

I watched the growing smiles on my parents' faces.

"Does this mean I can go?"

"It means you have a lot of work to do before we can give you our final permission," Abby said.

"But if we get more information and everything checks out okay, then the answer is yes?" I asked, trying to keep from jumping up and down in my seat.

"That's about the size of it," my dad teased.

"Whoopee!" I shouted, pushing back from the table. "I'm going to go call the others right now."

After three quick phone calls, I found out that the other girls' parents felt pretty much the same way that mine did. They wanted more details and a schedule. I wrote a letter to Patty telling her to save some time for us just in case we got to New York. I sealed and stamped the letter, and then I put it in the mailbox. *Further planning would have to wait*, I thought.

The next day, we had a big party to give. When we are in school, we only give parties on the weekends. But, oh, what weekends they are! Our schedule had been filled for three months. We usually do at least two parties each weekend. Sometimes, if we feel really ambitious, we'll do four parties over a weekend.

Last week, we did a super party for the children's ward at the hospital. Aimee's friend, Graham, had helped us by doing some special tricks for the kids. We performed a play about the holidays. Everyone seemed to have a lot of fun. Even the nurses looked like they were having a good time.

This weekend, we're doing a cookie theme party for Jackie Klein's third birthday. She is our youngest customer yet. We did a rainbows-and-flowers party for her big sister, Amanda, when she turned five last summer. Mrs. Klein asked us to do the party at my house, because theirs was being painted.

The next morning, the gang came over early to set up for Jackie's party. We decorated with pictures of the Cookie Monster's big blue face and hung blue and white streamers from the corners of the room. Aimee drew chocolate chips on the tan balloons to make them look like cookies.

The kids began to arrive. There were six kids at the party. They were all three and four year olds, except five-year-old Amanda. I handed out name tags at the front door, while Krissy put on her clown costume and Aimee got her craft supplies ready.

"Hi, Andrea," I said, safely pinning a light blue name tag in the shape of the Cookie Monster onto her overalls. Why don't you go over to Linda Jean, and visit with the bunny? She is soft and furry just like the Cookie Monster."

Andrea headed off in Linda Jean's direction to pet Regina, the angora rabbit. I put name tags on Sandy, Jeffrey, and Christopher. After I finished giving them their name tags, I directed each one toward Linda Jean.

Since we were entertaining three year olds, we planned a much shorter party than we usually give. This one was only an hour, with quick, easy projects and lots of entertainment to keep the kids happy. We had made a Cookie

Monster cake with blue frosting.

"Okay, everyone. It's time for the clown!" Krissy announced, coming out of the bedroom wearing her blue wig. She had a plastic bag tied loosely around her neck with a picture of a cookie taped onto the front.

"Are there cookies in there?" Andrea asked.

"Well, let's see." Krissy dug around inside the bag for a few seconds, and then she stuck her head into the bag, too. "How about this?" she asked, pulling out a long scarf. "Maybe there is a cookie at the end of it!"

While I left to change into my dance outfit, Krissy had one child after another try to pull the string of tied-together scarves out of her bag.

Once inside the bathroom, I quickly drew dark dots on my face and arms. I pulled the big brown sheet over my head that I had cut and sewn up to form the shape of a giant cookie. My brown tights stuck out of the bottom of my costume.

Aimee and I had prepared a neat song and dance that we would perform together for the children. She would sing, and I would dance. I stood in the hallway watching Krissy as she finished her clown act. The kids all were giggling at her funny tricks.

Aimee motioned for me to go back into the living room. "Now, everybody stand in a circle, and hold hands," she instructed.

I joined the circle, and we began walking around and around. Aimee and I started singing.

"Oh, I wish I was a cookie, a cookie, a cookie.
Oh, I wish I was a cookie, so big and so fat.
I would eat myself for breakfast, for breakfast, for breakfast.
I would eat myself for breakfast and then take a nap."

I danced around, taking pretend bites of my cookie costume. All of the kids laughed.

"Do you want a piece?" I asked Jackie as I pointed to my costume.

I broke off a pretend piece of my cookie costume and handed it to her. She ate the imaginary piece. Soon all the kids were having pretend bites of my costume. We sang the song over and over. Each time we said "nap," I fell on the floor, and all the kids fell on top of me pretending to be asleep.

After five nap times, I said, "This cookie

wants to eat for real."

"Yeah!" the kids agreed.

We ushered them over to the table for cake and ice cream.

"What kind of a party are we going to give for Alissa O'Toole?" Linda Jean whispered. "She's the same age as we are. She's not going to be interested in most of the themes we usually do, like teddy bears and unicorns."

"And she certainly wouldn't want a cookie monster theme," Aimee said, coming up behind us.

I laughed, danced around in a circle, and sang, "Oh, I wish I was a cookie..."

"I can just see it," Linda Jean said. "We'll have to think up something great for Alissa. It will have to be something that we've never done before, something that she'll never ever forget!"

Three

"I can't believe it. It's really happening!" I yelled as I jumped up and down in my living room. "We're going to New York!"

The Forever Friends sat in my living room facing all of our parents. This was the family meeting that Abby had said we needed before getting the final okay. She had invited all of the girls and their parents over to share their ideas and questions about the trip.

"I think it's time we call Mrs. O'Toole and make sure of the details. We want to be sure she's really willing to watch out for all of you," Mr. Jacobs said.

Abby dialed Mrs. O'Toole's number. While she was talking to Alissa's mom, I turned to my friends.

"Hey, what do you think about Abby coming along on our trip?" I whispered. "I hope the O'Tooles don't feel it's an imposition to bring one more guest."

"I'm sure they'll understand. The O'Tooles may be rich, but they're still parents," Linda Jean reasoned.

"You're right," Aimee said. "Let's pretend that it's all set and that we are going. What all do we need to take with us?"

The other parents wandered off into the dining room for coffee and snacks while Abby continued to talk on the phone. I didn't want to listen, but I found myself straining to hear every word Abby said to Mrs. O'Toole.

"Quit eavesdropping," Krissy said. "Let's make lists of clothes and stuff that we need to take to New York."

"What about costumes?" I asked. "We need to figure out what kind of party to have so we know what to wear."

"Do you think we'll need dress up clothes to go out shopping or to the theater?" Linda Jean asked. "Do you think they ever wear grubbies in New York?" She glanced down at her jeans with a worried expression.

"Of course, they wear grubbies in New York," I said uncertainly. I glanced over at Abby, who was still deep in conversation with Mrs. O'Toole. She was smiling and nodding her head. That looked like a good sign. "I wish I knew what she was saying."

"We're going. I can feel it," Aimee said.

"Madam Aimee predicts the future," I said, giggling. "Madam Aimee, tell me, will we meet any cute guys in New York? Will our names be up in lights on Broadway?"

Aimee put her fingers on either side of her head and swayed from side to side. She closed her eyes tightly and pretended that she was concentrating. Finally, she said, "Every time I try to picture a cute guy, all I see is Graham."

"You would," I said, giving her a playful shove. Graham is Aimee's friend who works at the television studio where her father hosts a local talk show. Just last week, we made Graham an honorary member of the Forever Friends Club after he performed with us for the children at the hospital. We all hoped he could help us out at more parties. The kids seemed to really enjoy his special tricks. And Aimee definitely liked having Graham around.

"I wrote a letter to my cousin Patty on Friday," I told them. "I hope we'll have time to see her while we're there. Maybe she can show us around New York if Alissa is busy."

"You should have plenty of time to get together with your cousin," Abby said, coming up behind us. "Because we're going to New York for seven fun-filled days and nights, courtesy of the O'Tooles."

"Yeah! All right! Cool!" we all shouted at once. Our excitement spilled over into the next room, and our parents came back in from the dining room.

"Mrs. O'Toole understood our concerns. She invited me to come along, too," Abby said with a big grin. "And they'll pay all our expenses."

"That's certainly very generous," Mrs. Lawrence commented.

"This is a wonderful opportunity for the girls," Mr. Branch remarked. Then he turned to us. "You girls will get to see lots of things that you'll never forget."

"Did Alissa's mom tell you what kind of theme she wanted for the party?" I asked. I couldn't wait to get started on the preparations.

Abby smiled. "Mrs. O'Toole said that Alissa wants to be surprised. She doesn't have any limit on what you should spend for the supplies, either."

Our parents went back to talking among themselves as we huddled together making plans. I wondered if Alissa would invite lots of show business kids to her party.

"We don't know much about Alissa, so it's hard to know what she'd like," Linda Jean said. "All I know about her is what I've seen in the movies."

"Yeah, and I didn't have a chance to talk to her very much when I met her in California," Krissy added.

"She seemed to like riding horses in *Shadow Stallion*," I recalled. "Maybe we should have a horse theme for the party. I could do a dance using galloping steps, and leaps and jumps."

"Or, Alissa might like something that has to do with pirates and buried treasure," Aimee mentioned. "Remember that movie she was in called *High Seas*?"

"Pirates would be an easy theme," Krissy remarked. "We could have a treasure hunt. I could pull coins from behind the guests' ears."

"But she was in an outer space adventure movie, too. And she was also in a comedy where she played a bratty younger sister. We really don't have any idea who the real Alissa O'Toole is," I said.

I lounged back on the couch. "Surprise her," I said, sarcastically, repeating Alissa's request. "What does that mean? I wish she had been more specific in what she wanted for her party. We can't do the little kid stuff because she is our age. Making blue fur party bags with googly eyes probably wouldn't excite her very much."

"I don't know about that. Jackie Klein's friends liked them," Linda Jean said and then laughed.

I made a face at her.

Krissy chewed on the eraser end of her pencil. "I have an idea," she said. "Alissa's mother said that money is no object, right? Well, let's give Alissa O'Toole a party she won't ever forget. We'll buy the expensive gold and silver streamers, helium balloons, and napkins printed with her name on them. How about a royalty theme? You know, like Alissa is the princess sitting on her throne, and we're the palace entertainment."

We all liked that idea. I immediately began imagining what music I could use and the dance I could do. I was thinking of a flowing costume with streamers and scarves that would flutter glamorously in the wind as I spun and twirled around.

Krissy said, "I could dress up as the court jester instead of a clown. I could still do my tricks. And maybe you could show me a few tumbling moves," she said to me.

"Sure. How's this?" I jumped off the couch, did a forward roll, and almost knocked over a lamp. "I'd better show you on the stage at school tomorrow instead."

It didn't take us long to finish the first stage of planning for the party. "Wow," Linda Jean said, looking at the figures Krissy had estimated for the cost of the party. "That's more than we've ever spent."

"Are you kidding?" I asked. "I think that's more than we've spent on all our parties put together."

"We'll have to buy the supplies in New York because we won't have room to take them on the plane with us. It's too much to carry," Aimee advised. "Last summer, when my family flew to Bermuda, we were only allowed to take two suitcases each."

"I'm going to pack all my clothes in one suitcase and bring another empty one along," Krissy told us. "I want to have plenty of room to bring back lots of souvenirs from the big department stores." We laughed.

Aimee put her hands up to her head again and closed her eyes tightly. Pretending to see the future, she said, "We are going to have a great time."

"I just hope Alissa likes her party," I said. "She's used to the best of everything. And I want Party Time to give her the best party ever."

Four

THE next few days flew by. Christmas shopping and gift wrapping took up lots of time during the first week of vacation. And we all spent every spare minute planning for our trip to New York. I couldn't believe that it was already time to start packing.

I looked at my list for about the hundredth time:

underwear

socks

leg warmers

leotards, ballet shoes, tights, dance skirt (for exercising and the party)

long-sleeved and short-sleeved shirts

sweaters (remember new one with sequins)

pants

new nightgown

dress for going out in the evening
warm hat and gloves

I just knew I was going to forget something.
My suitcase lay open on my bed. I put the green
zipper pouch with my toothbrush, toothpaste,
brush, barrettes, and perfume into the lower
right corner. Abby was packing our hair dryer
in her suitcase.

I called Linda Jean to see if she was packed.

"Are you ready yet?" I asked her when she
answered. "There's no way I'm going to be able
to sleep tonight."

"I know what you mean. I haven't even
started packing yet," she told me. "Percival has
a cold, so I had to make an emergency trip to
the vet's house since his office is closed today.
And Mac is throwing a fit." Percival and Mac
are Linda Jean's birds, a parrot and a macaw.
She has all kinds of animals, but her birds
are her favorites.

"Do you think they'll survive without you
for a week?"

"They'll be fine. Dad's great around all the
fur and feathers. It's Stephanie who I'm
worried about."

"Stephanie? Your stepsister?" I asked jokingly. It wasn't very long ago that Linda Jean was really upset about her mom and new stepfamily moving to Atlanta. She had been determined not to like her new stepbrother and stepsister.

"Yeah, I know it sounds weird. I can't believe we get along so great now. I was over at my mom's house for Christmas dinner, and Stephanie wouldn't stop crying. She said she was going to miss me so much while I'm in New York."

"That's cute. Steph really is a sweetheart. Did you finally get her calmed down?"

"Yeah, I finally did," Linda Jean said. "I had to promise I'd call her and write her from New York. I even told her I'd bring her back a surprise."

"I'll help you look for something for her if you want," I offered.

And then I heard Abby call me from the kitchen.

"Well, I'd better get going. I'll see you tomorrow," I said. We said good-bye and hung up.

Later that night, I got into bed, expecting to stay awake all night long. But the next thing I knew, my alarm clock was ringing loudly in my ear, and Abby was singing in the shower.

The airport was a jumble of lights and noise and people scurrying back and forth. This was the first time I had been on an airplane, and I was just a little bit scared. But I was so excited that I could hardly wait for the plane to take off.

We all were wearing our Forever Friends Club sweatshirts because they made us easy to spot in a crowd, and we knew it would be cold in New York.

The pilot came on the intercom a few minutes after we had taken off. "Good morning, ladies and gentlemen. Welcome to Flight 609 with direct service to New York City," he said.

"I'm glad we're on the right plane," Aimee joked, leaning over toward me.

"Well, it's too late now, anyway. We're way up in the clouds already, and I'm not jumping," I told her. "Hey, switch seats with me. I want to see out the window for a minute."

"The flight attendant said we have to stay in our seats until the seat belt sign goes off," Aimee reminded me.

I relaxed and listened to the pilot talking on the intercom.

"We are on schedule and due to land at La

Guardia Airport at one o'clock. Our approximate flying time will be an hour and 55 minutes. The weather in New York City is a cold 32 degrees, and a storm front is moving in. It looks as if New York's going to get some snow by this afternoon. I hope everyone brought their mittens."

"Mittens!" Krissy cried. "Oh, no. I forgot my mittens."

"Don't worry, Krissy," Abby assured her from across the aisle. "We'll buy some for you when we get there."

The seat belt light went off, and Aimee and I switched places. I couldn't see much, though. The airplane was already flying above the clouds. After a while I got tired of looking at the puffy white formations and began gazing around at the other passengers.

Aimee, Abby, and I were sitting in the three seats on the left side of the airplane. Linda Jean and Krissy were sitting across the aisle. Next to Krissy sat a woman with a little girl asleep on her lap.

In front of Linda Jean and Krissy was a family with two children, and I could hear two kids in the seats behind us.

"Boy, there sure are a lot of little kids on

this flight," I commented.

"It must be because of the holiday season. A lot of families are probably going to visit relatives," Abby said.

"Or, they might be going home after already visiting relatives," Aimee pointed out.

I pushed the button on the arm of my seat and leaned back until the seat reclined. "It's much more comfortable this way," I said. "I think I'll take a nap."

I had just closed my eyes when the kids in the seats behind us broke into a fight.

"Mom said I could sit by the window!" the boy shouted.

"But you got out of your seat!" the girl yelled back.

"I just went to the bathroom. That doesn't count as getting up."

"It does so!"

"Does not!" he yelled louder.

"Does so!" she retorted.

I turned around and looked over the top of the seat. "Why don't you take turns sitting by the window?" I asked quietly. "You know, 10 minutes for one of you and 10 minutes for the other?"

"Who asked you?" snapped the boy.

"Yeah!" added the girl.

I turned and faced forward again.

"Well, at least they're on the same side against you," Abby said, laughing.

Shrugging my shoulders, I said, "I was only trying to help."

After that, I must have fallen asleep. I know it seems weird since it was my first plane trip and all, but I must have been tired from all the preparations. I woke up to Aimee shaking my arm.

"Hey, guess what?" she asked excitedly as I put the headset back into the seat pouch in front of me. "The airport is all backed up because of the snow storm. We're circling around in a holding pattern until they clear the airport traffic jam."

I sat up and looked out the window. We were out of the clouds, and I could see that the ground was white with snow. The tiniest twinge of worry pricked at my insides. "How is the pilot supposed to land in this mess?" I asked.

The pilot's voice came over the intercom again. "Hi, folks," he said. "The snow is putting us a little behind schedule, but our visibility is still good. We should have you down in the the big city of New York in less than an hour. Currently, we're holding at 15,000 feet, about 40 miles from the city. Just sit tight, and the flight attendants will be available if you need anything."

"It's going to be another hour," Krissy moaned. "Where is solid ground when you need it?"

"At least we weren't sent to Philadelphia or Boston like some of the other airplanes were," Abby said calmly. She had tuned her headset into the tower channel so she could hear the pilots talking with the radio tower. "It's better that they take their time and get everyone down safely."

"I know," I said. "I'm just so excited about seeing New York. I don't want to wait another minute."

I looked around and saw that I wasn't the only restless passenger. Some people were looking anxiously out the windows, while others were busy gathering up their purses and briefcases. But it was the kids who were especially ready to land and get out into some fresh air.

The plane ride had been quiet up until the pilot's announcement. People had been reading, sleeping, or talking in low voices. But now the loud shrieks of frustrated children filled the air. The kids behind us were the loudest.

One of the flight attendants poked her head out from behind the curtain, surveyed the wiggling, squirming mass of little people, and ducked back inside.

"We have to do something," Aimee whispered. "These kids are getting out of hand."

"Did you bring any tricks with you?" I asked Krissy.

"I brought my rings and scarves, and a deck of cards," she replied. "I thought if our luggage got lost I'd at least have a few things to practice with."

"We can sing, too," Linda Jean said. "We don't need anything for that."

"Excuse me," I said to the flight attendant who was walking by our seats. "Do you mind if we gather a few children together near the front seats to sing songs? It might help to calm them down."

"That would be great," she said, looking relieved. "You can use the couple of vacant seats up front until the pilot gives the signal for final approach."

"Okay, here goes," Aimee said, leaning over

the back of our seats.

"How about a song?" she asked the kids, her voice surprising them. "Come on. Let's go up front. We have something to show you."

We took turns performing mini-versions of our Party Time acts. The four kids who gathered around us seemed to enjoy the show. They especially liked Krissy's card tricks.

But before we knew it, the pilot's voice came over the loud speaker again. "Please put your seat belts on. We have clearance and are on our final approach to the runway. And, thank you, girls," he added.

I sat down quickly, looking around. "Was the pilot listening the whole time?" I asked Aimee.

She pointed to the intercom above our heads. "Probably."

"Thanks. That was a wonderful job," a flight attendant said as she passed our row.

"You're welcome," we said.

"Well, this is it," I announced to myself more than to anyone else. "We're really landing in New York City."

I thought nothing could be more exciting than watching the city appear in the distance. The snow was falling less heavily. We saw the outlines of skyscrapers poking through the layers of swirling snow. The blue lights of the runway came up to meet the plane.

I couldn't wait to get off the plane and start exploring. I wondered if Alissa would be there to meet us. What would she be like? Would we like her? And what adventures lie ahead for us in the big city?

Five

AS we walked from the tunnel that takes passengers from the airplane to the main part of the airport, I let my eyes take in everything around me. We rode the escalators down to where the luggage comes in from the airplane.

The La Guardia Airport in Queens, which is a suburb of New York City, seemed to be much smaller than the airport in Atlanta. I bet you could live in the Atlanta Airport, and nobody would notice. Here, just a few shops lined both sides of the walkway.

"There's Hoffritz Knife Shop," I said, pointing to the window full of Swiss Army knives, professional cooking knives, and scissors. We use Hoffritz knives for all of our chopping.

Abby looked at the display. "I wish we had

time to stop, but Alissa must be worried about us by now."

"Will you recognize her?" Linda Jean asked Krissy.

"I think so. And I told her we would be wearing our Forever Friends sweatshirts. She should be able to spot these shirts anywhere."

We picked up our luggage (Aimee really did have one empty suitcase) and looked around, but there was still no Alissa.

"Let's go out front. Maybe she's waiting for us there," Abby remarked.

The airport lobby was filled with holiday crowds. I began to wonder if it was possible to find anybody in the pack of people.

"Excuse me," a woman in a dark uniform said to Abby. "I am the O'Tooles' chauffeur. Are you Abby Marshall?"

"Yes, I am. And this is Joy, Aimee, Linda Jean, and Krissy."

"I'm so glad I found you in this crowd," the chauffeur said. "My name is Denise. Please follow me."

She took one of Abby's suitcases and led us successfully through the mob of people toward the front doors.

"Is Alissa here?" I asked, eagerly. I was so

excited to see the star in person.

"I'm sorry. Miss O'Toole had a dance lesson and was unable to meet you in person. She will be waiting for you at the estate."

Linda Jean and I glanced at each other. I felt like royalty already.

After putting our bags in the trunk of the limousine, the chauffeur held the door open for all of us. We climbed gingerly into the biggest limo I had ever seen. There were four sets of seats besides the driver's seat. The two middle seats faced each other.

I settled back into the luxurious seat, breathing in the wonderful scent of leather. I ran my hands over the velvety walls of the limo.

"Wow!" Aimee exclaimed.

"Double wow!" I repeated.

I jumped when the smoky glass window rolled down between us and the driver. "Please feel free to have a snack from the tray on the table or something to drink from the refrigerator. Alissa keeps a supply of fresh juices and sparkling mineral waters," Denise said. And then she added, "It's about an hour's drive to the O'Toole estate in the Hamptons."

"Well, I'm hungry," I told them. I lifted the lid on the serving tray. A platter of meats, cheeses, condiments, and relishes was underneath. Curly leaves of lettuce rimmed the platter.

"What's in here?" Krissy asked, uncovering a napkin-lined basket.

"Oooh, bagels," she said, reaching for one.

Abby opened the small refrigerator that was tucked behind a curtain. She brought out five frosted, crystal goblets and opened a bottle of sparkling grape juice.

"I think I'm in heaven," Linda Jean whispered. "Do you think this is supposed to be lunch? Or, should we save some room for another meal at Alissa's?"

Abby looked at her watch. It's already two o'clock. They probably won't be serving a meal until dinner."

"That could be nine o'clock. I've heard that rich people eat late," Aimee mentioned.

"Why don't we ask Denise? She may know what the O'Tooles have planned," Krissy added.

I leaned forward and knocked on the glass partition. Denise's voice came over a tiny intercom hidden in the plush wall. "Yes, ma'am. What can I help you with?"

"We wondered if we should save room for

lunch, or if we should go ahead and eat now?"
I asked.

"The O'Tooles rarely have a sit down lunch.
So, if you're hungry, I would say to go ahead
and eat now. They usually serve dinner around
eight o'clock."

"Thanks. Uh, Denise?" I continued.

"Yes?"

"None of us have been to New York before,"
I told her. "Would you mind telling us some
of the sights that we'll be seeing on our way
to the estate?"

"I'd be happy to. I've lived in New York all my
life, and I'm proud to show off my home. Do
you mind a little detour so I can show you
some of my favorite places?"

"You're the driver," Krissy said.

"Yes, I am," Denise joked back.

Riding in the limo was fun. We ate and
gawked out the window at the City Corp
Building's angular shape. We saw the Empire
State Building and the United Nations Building.

"I wish it wasn't snowing so much. I can
barely make out the buildings," I commented.

"You're the one who wanted to go sledding,"
Krissy said.

"I want the snow to be on the ground, not in the air," I said.

"The weather report said the storm should blow over by tomorrow," Denise told us.

"That's great. I'm just dying to see everything," I added.

"I know what you mean. But don't worry. There's lots of time to look around," Denise said.

A while later, Denise pointed to the huge bridge we were approaching. "This is the 59th Street Bridge," Denise said. "You know, the one that the Simon and Garfunkel song was named after?"

"Who are Simon and Garfunkel?" Aimee asked.

Abby and Denise laughed. "They were a singing group before your time," Abby said. "But I have a few of their records at home if you're ever interested in going back in time a little."

Busy city streets gave way to long stretches of snow-covered country roads without houses. We sat back in comfortably-stuffed silence and watched the snowy fields go by. Every now and then we spotted a huge house through the whiteness. I felt my eyes drifting shut again.

"I think we're here," Aimee said.

I looked out the window and down the tree-lined drive.

"Is this their house?" I asked Denise, sitting up.

"This is it," she replied. "It's 400 acres' worth. They have a stable full of thoroughbred racehorses and plenty of room to ride them. I'm sure Miss O'Toole will want to show you around the grounds herself," she added.

The house was even more impressive than the land around it. "It's like something out of a storybook," Aimee said. "Look at that tower. I can just imagine a princess being held prisoner in there."

Denise drove the limo up to the front door. Several servants came down the wide marble steps to assist us with our bags. I looked at their crisp black and white uniforms. I looked down at my sweatshirt, my jean jacket, and my old blue jeans. I felt really grubby.

I touched my face. I was probably grimy from traveling, too. My teeth felt like they needed brushing, and I was sure my hair was messy. And here I was getting ready to meet a movie star.

The others probably felt the same way I did.

Krissy kept looking at me as we walked along behind the butler into the parlor.

"Mrs. and Miss O'Toole will receive you now," the butler said.

He slowly and expertly opened the formal double doors that led into the parlor. "Your guests have arrived, madam." Then he bowed ever so slightly to us on the way out. It was just like something out of an old movie.

Across the room sat Alissa and her mom. They looked so small sitting together on a couch across the big room. Alissa got up and took a step toward us.

"Oh, I'm so glad you're finally here," she said, clapping her hands. "Hi, Krissy. It's great to see you again." Her mother put a hand on her arm, and she sat back down.

"Welcome," Mrs. O'Toole said, standing up and extending her hand to Abby and then to each of us in turn. "I am Charlotte O'Toole, and this is my daughter, Alissa."

Abby introduced the rest of us, and one by one we shook Alissa's hand. It was all so formal that I almost laughed, but I could tell this was serious business to Alissa's mom.

The more I looked at Alissa and her mom in their perfectly-pressed dresses with their perfect hair, the more uncomfortable and grungy I felt.

Mrs. O'Toole looked at Alissa and nodded her head formally.

"I hope that your journey here was pleasant and that the drive from the airport was not too tedious," Alissa said. Her hands were clasped tightly in her lap, and she sat stiffly on the sofa.

Krissy spoke up. "The flight was fun, Alissa. We couldn't land for a while because of the snow. So, we gave a small party for the kids who got cranky from all the waiting."

"Really?" she asked, her eyes lighting up. "That sounds exciting. Did it work?"

"Yeah, the kids all seemed to have fun. We just sang a couple of songs to keep them busy. I did some easy magic tricks. It was fun," Krissy told her.

"I'm sorry I couldn't meet you at the airport. Mother thought it was best, with all the people and everything, that I stay home today and wait for you here."

"Yeah, it was pretty crowded," I told her.

"It's such a bother when Alissa is recognized," Mrs. O'Toole explained. "If she had come to meet you at the airport, you would probably still be there waiting as she signed autographs."

Mrs. O'Toole laughed at her own joke, but I wasn't sure she really thought it was funny. We all laughed, too, to be polite.

The doors opened behind us, and the butler entered carrying a folding tray and another platter of food.

"Refreshments are served, madam," he announced.

"Please help yourselves," said Alissa. She reached forward and picked up a cup and saucer. She filled the cup from the teapot. "Would anyone like some wassail?" she offered.

"What's wassail?" Aimee asked.

"It's hot apple cider and pineapple juice with cinnamon sticks," she replied. "Try some."

Each of us took a cup and tried to balance the cup, saucer, and plate of cookies on our laps. *Alissa must have had a lot of practice at this,* I thought. She had no trouble juggling all the food and talking at the same time.

"So, how was the weather in Atlanta when you left?" Alissa asked after we had organized our plates.

"It was cold and rainy," Abby said.

"I'm glad we're here," I told Alissa. "I'd like

to go sledding."

Everyone looked at me.

"If we have time, that is," I added as I shoved a cookie in my mouth. I hoped the whole week wasn't going to be like the first meeting. Because if it was, I could tell I'd better learn to think before speaking around here.

"Mother," Alissa said after a few more minutes of uncomfortable conversation. "Didn't you want to show Mrs. Marshall your orchids in the greenhouse?"

"Why, yes, I did. Would you like a tour, Mrs. Marshall?"

"That would be lovely," Abby said, grinning at us. "But please call me Abby."

"Oh, yes, and do call me Charlotte," Mrs. O'Toole said as they left.

We all looked at Alissa. She waited until the door was shut and we could no longer hear their voices or footsteps.

Suddenly, Alissa jumped up off the couch and plopped down on the floor in front of us. "Thank goodness she's gone," she said. "If I had to be serious like that for one more minute, I was going to burst!"

Six

A LISSA seemed to become a different person when her mother left the room. Just a few minutes before, she had been proper and polite, almost like a statue. She didn't seem like a kid at all.

But she was totally different when her mom left the room. It took us all a few minutes to get used to the new Alissa. *Which one was real?* I asked myself.

"Wait until you see what I have planned for us," she said. "Of course, we'll have to ditch Mother. But I'm sure I can figure out a way to do that. We'll go shopping. I know this great place. My mother would never go there, but it's my favorite place. Just wait. You've never seen so many clothes!"

We all must have been staring at her in

disbelief because she laughed, jumped up, twirled around, and sat down in front of us again.

"Fooled you, didn't I?" she asked. "You thought I was stuffy and boring?"

One by one, we got down on the floor with Alissa. "Actually, we thought you were very nice," Aimee said politely.

"Oh, come on," Alissa teased. "I saw your faces. You wanted to escape."

"It's true," I said finally. "I was wondering if we would fit in. I'm not used to all this formal stuff. I feel like I'm visiting a queen. I hope that doesn't make you angry."

"Are you kidding? I do anything I can to escape all this stuff myself. One time I even sneaked out in disguise and went to Coney Island to ride the roller coaster.

We listened in awe as Alissa told story after story of forbidden subway rides, shopping in bargain basements, and cab rides around the city.

"This week is going to be great! We'll go sledding like you wanted, Joy. We have a long hill out back behind the house. You're a science nut, aren't you, Linda Jean? Then we'll go to the Museum of Natural History. And we'll visit the Greenwich Village galleries for Aimee. How about you, Krissy? Where do you want to go?"

"How do you know so much about us?" I asked her.

"I had my mom ask your mom when they were talking. I wanted to be sure there were lots of great things to show you!" she said with an excited grin.

Boy, was this girl different from the one we'd met a few minutes earlier! Alissa was too much. I had never seen anyone move so fast and think up so many schemes at one time.

"There's only one problem. There's something I have to do. I can't get out of it," Alissa said.

"What's that?" I asked curiously.

"It's the ballet. I have to make this dumb appearance at the New York City Ballet's performance on Thursday."

"That's the day before your party, isn't it?" Krissy asked.

"Yeah. Boy, do I wish I could get out of it," Alissa added with a sullen expression coming over her face.

"What's wrong with going to the ballet?" I asked. "I'd love to go. In fact, I was hoping to get a chance—"

Before I had a chance to finish, Alissa covered her mouth with her hand. "Hurry, get back on the chairs," she said.

Just as we all settled once again onto the elegant cushions, the double doors swung open. Mrs. O'Toole and Abby walked in.

I glanced over at Alissa, amazed that she had heard their approach. She was perfectly posed on the edge of her seat like before they had left to tour the garden. She even had the teapot in her hand getting ready to pour another cup of wassail. What an actress!

"I can see that you girls are having a nice time getting acquainted, but I'm sure our guests are tired from their flight. Margaret, the upstairs maid, will show you all to your rooms so that you can freshen up before dinner."

"Dinner will be served at eight o'clock sharp," Alissa added, standing up. "The bell will ring twice, and then Margaret will show you to the dining room."

In a flash we were whisked away from the parlor and taken to our rooms by Margaret, a tall, thin woman with a nice but formal smile.

"If there is anything you need, just push the

red button on the panel," she told us, pointing to a board full of buttons.

"Would anyone mind if I made a local phone call?" I asked Margaret. "My cousin lives near here."

"I'm sure that wouldn't be a problem. Just press one of the lines that isn't being used. The lighted button means someone is on that line."

"Can you believe this place?" I asked Linda Jean after I had thanked Margaret and she had left. "They have a button panel for calling the servants and everything." I ran my fingers over the 10 buttons on the gold-plated panel. "I wonder what all these others buttons are for?"

"Don't push them. You're liable to find out," Linda Jean warned.

We took a while to survey our room. Linda Jean and I were sharing one room, and Aimee and Krissy were next door. A bathroom connected the two rooms. Abby had her own room across the hall from us.

"Our room is so beautiful," Linda Jean said. She ran to the window and pulled open the drapes. "Joy, look at this view!"

I took off my shoes and did a little waltz

step over to the window. My feet sunk into the fluffy white carpet.

"That must be the sledding hill that Alissa was talking about. And there are the stables," I said, pointing out beyond the rose garden and the gazebo.

"Where are our suitcases?" she asked, breaking into my thoughts.

"I don't know."

We looked around under the two matching four-poster antique beds, behind the floral print over-stuffed chairs, and around the matching mirrored vanities with velvet stools.

"Did you try looking in the closet?"

"Where *is* the closet?" she asked.

"What is that cupboard over there?" I asked, pointing to a huge carved oak piece.

"Let's look," she replied. Together, we pushed back the huge door. Sure enough, when we opened the doors, there were our clothes. They were all folded, and our dresses were ironed perfectly.

"This must be one of those old-fashioned wardrobes. I could get used to this kind of life," Linda Jean said, lying back on the bed.

"Me, too," I agreed. "What should we do now? We don't have to put our clothes away. Do you think we are supposed to dress up for dinner? I only brought one dress."

"I'm going to wear the new pants I bought last week. How about giving Patty a call now?" Linda Jean suggested.

"That's a good idea. Where's the phone?"

After a quick search, I located the antique-looking wooden phone on the wall next to the closet. I got out my address book and turned to find Patty's number. I dialed and waited.

"Hi, Patty. This is Joy," I said when she answered after only one ring. "We're here in New York, and you should see the place where we're staying."

"You know what?" Patty asked. "I think I only live a few miles from the O'Tooles'. We're practically in the same neighborhood."

"How do you like the big city?" I asked. I had to stand on tiptoe to speak into the black mouthpiece on the wall.

She sighed. "I haven't gotten around much yet. We're still settling in, unpacking and stuff."

"You mean you haven't even been sightseeing yet? That's terrible. Maybe you can go with us," I said.

"I'd like that, but I don't want to impose,"

Patty said softly.

"I'll find out what the schedule is and call you tomorrow morning. We could meet someplace neat like Macy's."

Patty put her hand over the phone and spoke to someone there. "Macy's is fine, but Mom wants to know if you could call me tonight to let me know for sure. We'll be up until 11:00."

"Okay, I will. Say 'hello' to your mom and dad for me. I'll talk to you later."

"I can't wait to see you, Joy," Patty said suddenly. "It's been a long time."

"Same here," I said. I hung up and turned to Linda Jean who had just finished writing a letter to Stephanie. "Now what should we do?"

Krissy and Aimee burst into our room. Have you seen the bathroom yet? Come look at our room," Aimee said.

First, we showed them around our room, and then we went back with them to theirs. On the way, we had to pause to stare at the bathroom.

"It's bigger than my whole bedroom at home!" I gasped.

"This *one* bathroom has two showers and four sinks! Do you think the O'Tooles have lots of parties?" Krissy asked.

"Are these really the guest rooms?" I wondered. "Or, do you think they lent us their own rooms?"

"I think this is the biggest house I've ever seen," Aimee commented. "I hope I don't get lost."

Aimee and Krissy's room wasn't like our room. Ours looked old and formal, and there were antiques everywhere. Their room was modern. There was enameled white furniture and glass chandeliers.

"Wow, I like this room, too!" I exclaimed. "I wonder what Abby's room looks like." I led everyone across the hall to my mom's room. She showed us around a room that looked like it came straight out of China. The decor was all red and black. There was a lot of oriental-looking artwork and decorations sprinkled everywhere.

"We have several hours before dinner," Abby told us. "Why don't you each take a shower and rest for a while? I'd like to do some reading."

Reluctantly, we trooped back to our rooms. There was no need to worry about running out of hot water at the O'Tooles' house. After we each took long steamy showers, we gathered on my bed to talk.

"Okay. We're now calling the first New York City meeting of the Forever Friends Club to order," Krissy said.

"That sounds neat," I told her. "Wouldn't it be fantastic if there were Forever Friends Clubs all over the world? I can see it now—the Amsterdam Forever Friends Club, the Iowa Forever Friends Club, the French Forever Friends Club. We could have pen pals and exchange neat party tips from all over the world!"

"Yeah, dream on," Aimee said. "But I do think we should continue having our regular daily meetings while we're here."

"That's a good idea. Let's get down to business. We're going to have to organize some kind of schedule. There are some things we need to do, like shop for supplies," Krissy put in.

"And there are some things Alissa is going to want us to do with her, like go sightseeing and all the other crazy things she has in mind," added Aimee.

"It's sounds as though Alissa is willing to do anything we want," commented Linda Jean.

"She's so lucky to be able to do all of these things."

"It's funny, though. She doesn't seem to be that happy with her life." I was thoughtful. "That comment about not wanting to go to the ballet was kind of strange. And she wasn't at all herself around her mother."

"That was strange, wasn't it?" Krissy remarked as she slid a comb through her hair and tried to yank out the tangles.

"But don't you think most kids act differently around their parents than when they're around their friends?" Aimee asked. "I think you two are jumping to conclusions."

"Well, I think it was more than just acting differently," I insisted. "I mean, who wouldn't want to go to the ballet if she had the chance?"

"Perhaps she just isn't as excited about the ballet as you are," Linda Jean said softly.

I unrolled the towel that was wrapped around my head and shook out my short hair. "Maybe you're right. And maybe you're wrong. I still think there is more to Alissa O'Toole than we think."

We spent the next two hours getting ready for dinner, resting, and doing the things we liked best.

I put on my leotard and did warm-up exercises to music. And then I danced around the spacious room. Aimee completed her needlepoint project of a bluebird. Krissy played solitaire and practiced her card tricks, while Linda Jean read her latest issue of *Young Scientist* magazine.

I glanced outside and saw Christmas lights reflecting on the fresh blanket of snow that surrounded the house. My stomach began to grumble. I wasn't used to such late dining hours.

Finally, the bell rang twice. Then there was a light knock on the door. I opened the door, and Margaret waited patiently outside.

"Supper will be served in 15 minutes. I will be happy to escort you downstairs," she said.

I felt just like one of the rich families on the nighttime soap operas on TV. What fun it was to be a part of this world!

Seven

"I'M so excited that Mother agreed to let me go shopping with you by myself," Alissa said the next day as we piled into the limousine. "Usually she goes with me or sends Margaret to watch what I do. I have to escape if I want to do anything fun."

"I'm sure your mother is just trying to protect you," Abby told her. "Mothers are like that." She looked over at me and smiled.

This morning, Alissa didn't look at all like the girl who had eaten a formal supper with us last night. At supper, she had been wearing a white lace dress with jewelry and fancy shoes. I was glad we had decided to dress up a little, too.

For our shopping trip, Alissa wore a disguise so that she wouldn't be noticed by her fans.

She didn't want to take up our sightseeing time by signing autographs. Her short brown hair was stuffed under a baseball cap. She had freckles penciled onto her nose and cheeks, and she wore a baggy sweatshirt with New York Yankees written across the front of it. She also wore a pair of faded jeans. I was sure that no one would recognize her.

The window rolled down between us and the driver. "Where to, Miss O'Toole?" Denise asked.

"What time is it, Denise?" Alissa asked her.

"It's just about 10:00," the chauffeur replied.

Alissa turned to us with a wink. "Are you guys up for a thrill? Let's go to the Fourstar Factory outlet for some exciting shopping you'll never forget!"

"Pardon me, miss," Denise interrupted. "But it's only two days after Christmas. Fourstar is likely to be rather crowded."

Alissa waved her hand to say it was okay. "Fourstar is always crowded. Besides, that's half the fun." She turned to me. "Don't worry. We'll still have time to meet your cousin at Macy's. I'm really glad you called her. I usually don't have anyone to shop with. Now I have a whole group!"

We settled back for the ride to the garment district. Along the way, Alissa entertained us with stories about famous people she knew.

"During one of the shows I did called *Best of Broadway*, I practically fell over Michael O'Shawnessy during one rehearsal. The director liked the move so much that he added it permanently to the show," she said. "Then I had to fall down every night for weeks."

When we finally stopped giggling, I asked, "Which do you like better, doing movies or performing live onstage?"

"Oh, the stage is my favorite!" she answered without hesitation. "I love hearing the crowd. When the show is live, you have to be better because you only get one chance. You can't believe how exciting a crowd can be."

"That's for sure," I said. "I remember the time I was dancing in *Sleeping Beauty* as one of the fairies. I kept messing up on one set of steps right up until the end. It was a balance with a *pas de bouree* and a *grand jete*. I just couldn't remember the steps, no matter how many times I practiced them."

"But when the lights dimmed and the curtain came up, you were fine, right?" Alissa asked, leaning close to me.

"It was a breeze then," I admitted. "There is something about knowing that a thousand people are counting on you that makes you perform well."

"I just wish I didn't have to do this ballet thing on Thursday," Alissa said and sighed.

By then I was feeling comfortable enough with Alissa to tell her what I thought. "You're crazy not to want to go," I said. "I would love to attend a performance by the famous New York City Ballet Company. Just to have the chance to go to Lincoln Center would be great." I sighed dreamily. "To me, it seems like the chance of a lifetime."

"It's just that I like musical comedy better," Alissa explained. "I know I have to take ballet and tap and jazz lessons for my acting, but that doesn't mean I have to like it."

"Well, just let me know, and I'll trade places with you anytime."

"I may just take you up on that," Alissa replied sadly.

I didn't have the chance to ask Alissa what she really meant by her last remark. The limo pulled up in front of the Fourstar in the midst of New York's garment district. In just seconds, we were swept from the comfort and luxury of our plush limo into the chaos and noise of one of the most famous bargain stores in the whole country.

"Come on," Alissa said. "If we happen to lose each other in this chaos, just meet at the front door in one hour."

In a flash, Alissa ran through the crowd of shoppers. I followed quickly behind her, trying to keep up. People were screaming. Clothes were flying overhead. Women were trying on garments in the aisles over leotards.

I picked up a purple sweater and held it up to me. "What do you think of this?" I asked my mom.

Before she had the chance to look, a lady grabbed it out of my hand. "That's mine!" she snarled.

"Are we actually supposed to shop here?" I yelled.

Abby shook her head in disbelief. "I don't know how you can find anything in here. Maybe you'll find something if you look around on the floor at the discarded items."

"That's just what I want to do, buy clothes that someone has trampled into the dust," I said sarcastically.

"You're a tourist, aren't you, honey?" a

woman next to me asked. "It's not usually quite this crazy in here. But today everything is 50 percent off. If you can stand it, you'll go home with the bargains of a lifetime."

"Thanks for the tip," I said, trying to manage a smile.

"Joy! Joy!" Alissa shouted, weaving her way through the packed aisles toward me. "Look what I found. It looks like it's your size!"

She held out a beautiful shimmering lavender leotard and a matching purple wraparound dance skirt.

"Oh, they're beautiful," I said, looking at the price tags. That's a good deal," I said. I'll go try on the outfit right now."

"Good luck getting into a dressing room. You're better off just slipping it on over your clothes. Or, buy it, and bring it back if it doesn't fit," Alissa suggested.

"Really? Okay." I looked at the size tag on the leotard. I knew it would fit me. I wrapped the skirt around my waist over my pants and decided to buy it.

"Can I buy it, Abby?"

"You better look around, and make sure it's what you really want," she replied.

I started to put the skirt back down on the

table, but Alissa grabbed my arm. "If you think you want it, don't put it down. It won't be there when you get back," she warned me.

"Okay. I'll carry it," I said as I moved on to the next table of clothes.

A second later, Aimee ran up to me with a coat she had found. Linda Jean was right behind her with some earrings and a pair of boots that she wanted to buy.

"I wish Atlanta had a place like this. I found shirts to embroider, and look at these great belts. I can paint designs on them." Aimee's arms were so loaded down that I had to laugh.

"Can you really afford all that?" I asked.

"Look at the prices. I can get all of this for what I would spend for one nice outfit at home."

It was easy to get excited by the craziness of the crowd. Soon we were searching around in the bins and racks like regular New York shoppers.

After an hour, we all decided to stay longer at Fourstar because there was so much to see. By the time we were ready to leave, we each had an arm load of great bargains. We dumped everything near the check out, and we quickly checked through our stacks to decide what to buy and what we could live without.

"Isn't this the greatest?" Alissa asked. She dropped an equally large pile next to ours. "What did you find?" she asked us, poking through our piles.

"Well," Aimee began.

"Oh, don't tell me. Let's just take them all home and give ourselves a fashion show," Alissa suggested excitedly.

"I hate to burst your bubbles, guys, but we're on a budget," Aimee said. "We have to save some of our allowances to buy souvenirs and maybe something really special later on."

"Didn't I tell you?" Alissa cried. "This shopping trip today is on me. Mother gave me her credit card and said to buy anything you wanted."

"That's very generous," Abby said. "But I don't think it's necessary. The girls brought their own money that they have earned doing parties. We certainly don't expect you to buy all these clothes."

But Alissa was already piling the garments we had selected onto the cashier's table. "I don't want to hear another word about it. I invited you, and I'm treating you to these things. It's fun for me!"

We looked on in awe as the numbers added up on the register. Before we knew it, Denise was loading the packages into the trunk, and away we went to Macy's.

We had a few Macy's stores around Atlanta, too, but I knew they weren't as big as the one in New York. I was expecting a super modern-looking building, but the store that we pulled up near was plain and old. It looked just like the other buildings along the busy street.

We quickly stepped from the limo into the rush of shoppers walking along the sidewalk.

"Where's Patty?" I asked, looking around the doorway.

"I hope she had sense enough not to wait out here," Alissa said. "Let's go inside and see if she's waiting there."

We stepped one by one into the revolving doors and walked in a circle until we were inside Macy's. The decorations, the people, and everything else looked like they were right from an exciting fairy tale. I was overwhelmed. I couldn't believe how gorgeous everything was. Flocked trees stood on every aisle and silver garlands decked with giant gold and silver balls draped from the ceilings, walls, and pillars. The decorations seemed to go on forever. But Patty was nowhere in sight.

"This is beautiful!" I exclaimed, letting out the breath I was holding. "But how will we find Patty in this huge place? Is there more than one entrance?"

"I think there are at least 10 doors to this place," Alissa informed me. "We'll have to check them all." She practically flew from one side of the building to the other. I could tell she had been here many times. We followed, looking up and down each aisle, but we still couldn't find Patty.

"You girls wait near the front entrance while I go telephone Bea," Abby suggested. "We'll find out when Patty left and how she was getting here."

She had only been gone a few minutes when Patty came spinning around the circular door. She shook off the snow from her coat and stuffed her mittens into her pockets. She saw me and ran over.

"I'm sorry I'm late," she said, hugging me. "I got lost, as usual. I took the wrong train and almost ended up in New Jersey. I had to double back, and I finally ended up taking a taxi."

"I'm glad you made it. We were so worried about you," I said.

I made quick introductions.

Alissa and Patty were about as different as two people could be. Alissa's hair was short and brown like mine. Patty had long and curly red hair and green eyes. Alissa's eyes were brown like mine. Alissa was short and petite, and Patty was tall and lanky. Alissa looked more like my cousin than Patty did.

Everyone hit it off right away.

"I haven't been around the city much since we moved here," Patty confessed. "I hate getting lost, and I always do."

"You need a crash course in getting around. Stick with me," Alissa said. "We'll get rid of my chauffeur, and I'll take you all on a tour of New York that you'll never forget."

Abby came back, and she smiled when she saw that Patty was standing with us.

The next few hours seemed to fly by. Alissa suggested that Denise go have lunch and meet us in six hours in front of Rockefeller Center.

"If you're sure," Denise had said uncertainly, looking at Abby.

"Don't worry. I'll take care of them," Abby said. "We're just going to shop." I don't think even Abby imagined what Alissa had in store for us.

First, we rode the old-fashioned wood-slat escalators up and down in Macy's. We oohed and aahed at the beautiful displays and the big prices on all the merchandise. Even though Christmas was over, the holiday spirit was everywhere.

A pretty glass ornament caught my eye on the half-price table. Alissa bought it in a flash. She made each of the other girls choose an ornament, too.

"Now every year when you decorate your tree, you'll remember your trip to New York," she said.

After Macy's, we went out a side exit, and Alissa led us past all the street people selling all kinds of things. We headed down to the underground subway station.

We took the direct train to Fifth Avenue. Alissa knew just where to get off. It was obvious that she had ditched Denise or her mother before and learned her way around on her own.

"I'm impressed," Patty told her. "All the stations look alike to me. I probably would have missed this stop."

"No problem. I've been doing this all my life. You just have to learn concentration and speed. Have you noticed that New Yorkers walk and talk faster than anyone on the planet?"

Patty laughed. "I sure have. New York is definitely faster paced than Rock Creek, Arkansas!"

"What's that like?" Alissa asked. She looked fascinated.

"The scenery is a lot like the Hamptons. There are rolling hills, streams, and trees."

"Except that in the Hamptons it's called landscaping. So, it's not really natural," Alissa said.

"I know. But at least it makes you feel like you're living in the country." She looked sad for a moment and blinked a couple of times like she was holding back tears.

"Why did your family move, Patty?" Aimee asked.

"My dad opened an office in New York. He's in the importing business," she explained. "He really tried to stay in Rock Creek, but he spent more time in New York than he did at home. So, we moved."

"My dad flies a lot, too," Alissa sympathized.

"Do you miss your old home very much?" Krissy asked Patty.

Patty wiped her eyes with her mittened hand. "I miss it every day. The kids at my new school aren't that friendly. They make fun of my accent. And I used to know my way around to go shopping by myself. Now I feel lost all the time."

Alissa listened quietly. "Well, cheer up," she said, putting her arm around Patty. "You're with friends now, and we're going to have a great time!"

We wandered down Fifth Avenue, joining the crowds around the store window displays. One window had a miniature ice rink with a warmly dressed skater circling on tiny skates. Another window had an entire Santa's workshop, complete with busy elves and reindeer stomping their hooves ready to be off with their sleigh full of packages.

We went to Saks Fifth Avenue and Bloomingdale's. We admired the huge decorated outdoor tree in Rockefeller Center and the 350-foot high spires of Saint Patrick's Cathedral. We spent our last hour skating on the outdoor ice rink with rented skates.

Somewhere along the way, we had given up trying not to let Alissa buy things for all of us. But we surprised her by treating her to a festive lunch at a little cafe near the ice rink.

After lunch, we piled back into the limousine for the ride home. We giggled and joked most of the ride back to the O'Tooles'.

"I'm exhausted," Aimee said. "I didn't think I could ever get tired of shopping or skating, but my feet are killing me."

"You'll feel better after a soak in the hot tub and dinner."

I held my stomach and moaned. "No more food, please! I think we sampled every food New York has to offer."

"That's the best way," Alissa said. "A bite here and a bite there. The street vendors are the best, though. They sell hot dogs and pretzels. Eating like that helps me keep up my energy. We'll try eating some stuff from the street vendors next time!"

"I have to admit you all have more energy than I do," Abby said, putting her stocking feet up on the opposite seat. "I'm ready for bed."

"But there's so much else to see in New York. I have lots more planned for tomorrow. It's too bad we can't go to the Bronx Zoo, but most of the animals are moved to warmer climates in winter. But we'll go to the Museum of Modern Art and the American Crafts Museum. We'll take in the Museum of Natural History and the Empire State Building. You just have to see the view from up there. You haven't been to New York if you don't climb to the top of King Kong tower."

"Climb?" I yawned. "Don't they have an elevator?"

"But it's much more fun to climb," Alissa insisted. "Just wait, you'll see what I mean. You come, too, Patty," she said as we dropped my cousin at her house, a small but elegant home only a few miles from Alissa's home.

"Thanks. I'd like that. And thank you again for all your gifts. I had the absolute best time today."

After she left, Alissa said, "You know Patty didn't mention my acting once today. Doesn't she know who I am?"

"She probably doesn't," I said, yawning again. "Patty reads much more than she watches TV or goes to the movies."

"Hmmm," Alissa said.

I fell asleep listening to Alissa O'Toole pack a week's worth of activities into tomorrow morning. It made me wonder if Alissa had any other friends to do things with. Why was she squeezing so much into the few days we were here?

Eight

AFTER our exhausting day, none of us felt like eating dinner. We managed to pick our way through the meal. But amazingly, Alissa ate two full plates of crab-filled pork chops, rice pilaf, and an incredibly beautiful spinach salad. I wondered where she got her energy—and her appetite.

"I hope you had a wonderful time shopping today," Mrs. O'Toole said, addressing everyone at the table. "I'm so sorry Mr. O'Toole couldn't join us tonight. He was called away early this afternoon to solve a problem at his London office."

"We had a splendid time, Mother," Alissa answered for us. "Will Father be back for my birthday party?"

"Of course, he'll be back, Alissa. I know he

wouldn't miss it for the world."

"He missed last year's party and the one the year before that," Alissa reminded her mother in a cool voice.

Mrs. O'Toole gave her a sharp look, and then she looked away. "You're neglecting your guests, dear."

It looked as if Alissa might say something, but she clamped her lips together and folded her arms.

"Why don't we all adjourn to the parlor. Alissa, don't you have a piece on the piano you would like to play for your friends?"

"Uh, yes. Certainly, Mother. Please follow me," she said, turning to us.

"Alissa, you don't have to play the piano for us," I said, coming up behind her. "We've all had a long day, and I'm sure no one would mind if you didn't play."

"It's quite all right, Joy. I enjoy the piano. You relax while I entertain you."

It wasn't so much what she said, but the way she said it that made me put my hand on her shoulder. "You don't have to do this," I whispered.

She shrugged my hand off. "Yes. Yes, I do." Her eyes looked blankly at me, and I knew better than to go on.

I watched Alissa closely as she performed *Beethoven's Ninth Symphony*. Her back was stiff. Her eyes were focused straight ahead, except for the slight smile she gave us at the beginning of her performance. *Where was the happy person who had raced us up the escalators at Macy's and who had spun us on the ice until we were completely dizzy?*

I glanced over at Mrs. O'Toole. She was smiling brightly as she watched her daughter.

Boy, Alissa really needs a chance to escape, I thought. *If only for a little while, she needs to be like a normal kid.* I perform because I like it. I like to dance. I like to be up onstage. But how would I like it if I had to pretend to be someone I wasn't in my very own home?

I was still thinking about Alissa's split personality when I went up to my room later to get a sweater. As I was coming back down the stairs, I overheard Alissa and her mother arguing.

"Leave me alone, Mother. I did what you wanted me to. I played the piano for my guests."

"I just want you to remember your obligation to the ballet this Thursday. You must go.

It is a great chance for your career. And, besides, the ballet company is counting on you."

I knew I should go back up the stairs and wait in my room until they were finished talking. But at the mention of the ballet, my feet became rooted to my spot on the stairs.

"I told you from the beginning that I didn't want to do the ballet thing," Alissa hissed. "I'm going to look like a fool."

"Your agent has gone to a lot of trouble to get you an appearance at the ballet. Just being seen there will bring in offers for new musical roles."

"I hate the ballet," Alissa almost screamed. "I don't want to be paraded around as a publicity stunt. I won't do it. I won't!" She stamped her foot.

"You will do it," her mother insisted.

"You can't make me," Alissa retorted.

"Yes I can. If you don't show up at the ballet, I will cancel your birthday party. I feel this is for your own good," she said, reaching out to Alissa.

But Alissa was already out of reach. I backed up into the shadows as Alissa ran past me crying loudly. A few seconds later, the door to her room slammed shut. Mrs. O'Toole squared her shoulders and marched back to the parlor. I sat on the top step, going over what I had heard, trying to understand what had happened.

Alissa didn't come back down to the parlor. After 15 minutes of trying to keep the conversation going with Mrs. O'Toole, Abby asked her if she would like to see the pictures in our party album. Abby seemed eager to have an excuse to leave us alone in the room.

"What are we going to do?" I asked, as soon as Abby and Mrs. O'Toole had left. "Alissa is really unhappy about this ballet she has to attend, but she's only doing it so she can have her birthday party."

"How do you know that?" Aimee asked.

"I overheard her and her mom arguing on the stairs. Alissa is in her room crying right now," I explained.

Then I told them the rest of the story, ending with Alissa slamming her bedroom door.

"I knew Alissa wasn't herself around her mom," Linda Jean said. "But I never dreamed she was this unhappy."

"Alissa needs us to be with her more than anything right now," I told them. "She sure doesn't need a fancy party that treats her like a princess. That's the part of her life that she hates."

"Alissa is such a nice person. She's generous and kind and friendly, too," Aimee said. "She remembered all the clerks by name in the stores we went to. And look at all the stuff she bought us. I wish we could do something for her that's really special, something that would make her happy."

"I've got it," Krissy said, jumping up. "Remember in the limo when Alissa was talking about all the stuff she can't do because she gets recognized? One thing she seemed really upset about was not seeing the circus."

"What if, instead of the fancy party we had planned, we do a plain, old-fashioned Big Top party?" I asked. "Forget the expensive decorations and the fancy costumes. I think Alissa would like an ordinary party more than anything else."

We put our heads together for a quick planning session. Krissy had brought her regular clown outfit with her just in case she ripped her fancy costume.

"I also have my regular bag of tricks," Krissy admitted. "I couldn't resist bringing them."

"It's terrific that you did," Linda Jean said. "I think I'll go investigate what's in the kitchen. My *Young Scientist* magazine had an article about creating magical chemistry with ordinary household products."

"Hey, that's a really good idea. I know I can think up a dance that uses tumbling and ballet, and maybe a little jazz and tap on the side. Who knows? Maybe Alissa will join me on-stage," I said.

"What can I do?" Aimee wondered. "I have plenty of songs about circus animals, but they're all so babyish."

"So what? Alissa never had the chance to be a kid. She's been too busy with her acting," I remarked. "What if you do the songs double time and add some hand motions? Alissa might like the challenge."

"Hmmm," Aimee murmured. "I think I have an idea for a craft at least. I'm sure I'll think of something."

"How many people are coming to this party?" Krissy asked. "Do you think they would mind if we invited Patty? She and Alissa seemed to get along really well when we were shopping."

"Let's ask Alissa about all of this tomorrow. Right now, I'm ready for bed," I said.

"We'll be up in a minute," Linda Jean said.

I headed up the stairs, the events of the day finally beginning to drag my muscles down. I guess Linda Jean was too excited about her idea to go to bed without checking out the kitchen immediately. And I could hear Aimee and Krissy trying to play a song on the piano.

I'll create my dance tomorrow morning, I told myself as I put one foot after the other on the stairs. All I wanted to do was sleep.

"Joy! I'm so glad you're alone," Alissa said as I entered my room. She was sitting on my bed with my family pictures spread around her.

She held a picture of Liza and Jeremiah. "Is this your sister?" she asked.

I couldn't be upset with her for looking through my things. She looked so sad and little as she sat cross-legged on my bed. I sat down next to her and pointed to the picture.

"Yeah, that's Liza. She's 23. Jeremiah is 10 months old now. This picture was taken a month ago."

"He's really cute. Do you baby-sit for him?"

"Every chance I get," I said proudly. "They live close to us, so we get to see them all the time. This is my other sister, Mary," I said, picking up another photo. "She just graduated from high school and moved into an apartment with two girlfriends. She doesn't come home as often as Liza does."

"Why?"

I smiled. "I think it's because she's trying to do everything on her own and prove that she's grown up."

One by one, I told her who the people in the pictures were. There were pictures of my dad, my grandmother before she died, a couple of the parties we had given, and Aimee, Krissy, and me when we were babies.

Alissa stacked the pictures silently and handed them back to me. "I wish I had a sister," she said. "There's no one to play with or talk to around here."

"What about friends? What about the kids who are coming to your party?" I asked softly.

"They're just coming because they have to, not because they want to. They are the other actors and actresses from the studio. I only see them at work and at my birthday party once a year."

"That's really sad," I told her. "I don't know what I would do if I didn't have my friends. There are some things you just can't talk about with your mother."

"That's for sure!" she said.

We looked at each other and started laughing. Suddenly, Alissa stopped laughing and stared at me. She pulled me over to the mirror.

"Look. We could be sisters. We're the same height. Our hair is almost the same length and color. Would you pretend to be my sister for the next few days? I could pay you to do it."

How could I resist? Alissa's eyes pleaded with me.

"Well, sure, I guess I could do that. But, Alissa," I said. "You don't have to pay me to be your sister or your friend. I like you the way you are. So do the others. We like you because you're such a nice person, not because you're a star or have lots of money."

She seemed stunned, as if friendship for its own sake was a new idea to her.

"Can I tell you a secret?" Alissa asked.

"Sure," I said.

"My mom always tells me that if you want something, you have to pay for it. She always tells people to put their money where their mouths are."

"That doesn't sound very tasty," I replied,

and then I grinned.

Alissa giggled. She bounced on the bed. "I've never really had a best friend," she told me. "I'm too busy to get to know people."

"You should make time for a friend. Maybe you need to give someone a chance."

"Like Patty?" Alissa asked.

"Exactly. Patty needs a friend as much as you do right now. You could really help her out. She's new to New York and confused about getting around."

"Hey, I'm good at getting around. I helped her today, didn't I?" Alissa asked, her face beginning to brighten.

"And she really appreciated it. Buying her presents was nice, but I know Patty pretty well. She wouldn't pretend to like someone no matter what they bought her," I said.

"I liked her, too. It's kind of nice to meet someone who hasn't seen me in the movies. I'm just another girl to her."

"Can I tell you a secret now?" I asked.

"Sure," Alissa said, folding her hands in her lap and waiting.

"It's my dream to see The New York City Ballet and someday to dance onstage with them. Most people think I'm silly," I confessed.

"Well, I don't," she said solemnly. Then her face brightened. "Hey, I have to do that ballet thing tomorrow. I have a great idea. Let's switch places. I'm sure you're a much better dancer than I am. No one would ever know."

"What? You want me to go watch the ballet in your place?" I asked.

"No, silly. I want you to take my place and *perform* in the ballet. No one will know we switched places because you'll be wearing a soldier costume. Your face will be covered. This is a perfect plan!"

"Wait a minute!" I said loudly, holding up my hand in protest. "I thought you were just going to watch the ballet and stand up to be recognized in the audience. I never dreamed you were actually going to be in the show."

"Oh, the dance is simple. You could learn the steps in an instant. You just told me that you've always wanted to dance with The New York City Ballet. Well, I'm giving you your chance to do that. Please help me out, Joy!" Alissa begged.

My head was spinning. Was Alissa serious? Did she actually think we could switch places and no one would ever find out? My conscience said "Say, no." My heart said, "Go for it!"

"Alissa, I really can't perform in your place at the ballet. But I'd love to go and watch. All of us would go and support you," I offered.

"Please, Joy. I just know I'll miss the steps. I feel so stupid dancing with all those professionals. Besides, they're only having me perform because my agent paid them, I'm sure. Weren't you telling the truth when you said people should like you because of who you are, not because you pay them?"

"Yes, but..." I continued to shake my head.

"You'd be doing me more of a favor than you realize. If you perform in my place, the dancing will be good. Mother will be happy. My agent will be happy. The ballet company will be happy that I didn't ruin their show. And I'll be happy because my reputation as a dancer will be great."

"But, it won't be you," I reminded her. "What if you get a bunch of offers for ballet parts—in case I'm terrific, that is? I won't be here every time you have to perform."

"But that's the beauty of it. Don't you see?" Alissa asked. "After this one performance, I can turn down offers because I don't want them, not because they think I can't dance the part."

"This is absolutely the craziest idea I've ever heard," I said.

"Does that mean you'll do it?" Alissa asked excitedly.

I looked in the mirror again at how Alissa's eyebrows curved exactly like mine. I noticed how her chin pointed slightly, making her face look heart shaped like mine.

"It means," I said. "That I'll think about it."

"Oh, Joy. It's so great having a sister to talk to." Alissa leaned over and hugged me.

Oh, boy, I thought in panic. *What have I gotten myself into?*

Nine

THE next day, I didn't have time to dwell on Alissa's crazy switcheroo plan. From the time we woke up, she had the Forever Friends and Patty on another whirlwind tour of New York and all its finest. We explored the museums and climbed the stairs of the Empire State Building. In spite of what Alissa had promised, though, I thought all those stairs were exhausting.

After dinner, we all went up to bed early. Every muscle in my body seemed to hurt. Abby went to take a long bath, but I just hopped quickly into bed and fell into a sound sleep. Knowing Alissa, she would be up and ready to go again early the next morning. And I wanted to be ready.

Sure enough, just after seven o'clock, the

bedroom door flung open.

"Are you up?" Alissa asked cheerily. "If anyone wants to go to rehearsal with me, we have to get a move on." She smiled at me and shut the door.

"Rehearsal? What is she talking about?" Linda Jean asked as she finished dressing.

I told her about the ballet, and about the long talk Alissa and I had had the night before last. I didn't tell her that I was thinking about dancing in the ballet for Alissa. I hadn't decided yet if I was really going to go through with it, and I wasn't ready to share the news.

We finished dressing and went down to breakfast. We had a busy day ahead of us, with all the decorating and new routines we had to practice.

"How long is rehearsal?" I asked Alissa across the table. "We still have to set up for the party."

"I know," Alissa said. "But I also want all of you to come watch me in the ballet tonight. I already had Mother reserve seats for you."

"And I thought just getting ready for the party was going to be enough for one day," Linda Jean moaned. "Oh, well. We have lots of energy, right?"

"I'm so glad you guys are coming to cheer me on tonight. We have to leave for rehearsal in 10 minutes." Alissa charged out of the room.

Linda Jean slipped her shoes on quickly. "I can't believe that girl," she said. "When I get home, I'm going to need a vacation from my vacation."

I was too nervous to comment. I knew I wasn't going to the theater to watch a rehearsal. I was going to learn a part that I would have to perform perfectly to a live audience that night.

I saw the Atlanta performance of the *Nutcracker* last Christmas, and now I sat desperately trying to recall the present-opening scene. I remembered that during the scene, there also were lots of other people milling around and opening gifts.

Panicky thoughts ran through my head all the way from the house to the theater. A part of me concocted a million excuses why I shouldn't do this for Alissa. But the other part of me was thrilled at this chance of a lifetime!

The theater had a special smell all its own. It was a combination of the well-worn velvet seat cushions, the carved wooden railings, and the heavy burgundy-colored stage curtain. My feet tingled in anticipation.

"We have the best seats in the house," Aimee commented. "Third row, center."

"I'm sure our view won't be this terrific tonight, so enjoy it now," I told them. In fact, I had hoped our seats would be in the highest balcony. Otherwise, Alissa's mother was sure to guess the truth.

I turned my attention to the action onstage. They were setting up the Christmas tree and the presents for the first act. Alissa went to talk to a cute blond guy wearing black stretch pants and a green tunic. Alissa's costume was gold and lavender with a dark purple sash. As I watched, the music began, and they each put on their soldier hats and shouldered their wooden guns.

One set of soldiers came forward with pointed toes, marching in time to the music. Alissa and the boy walked out together. The boy knew his steps, but Alissa kept flubbing hers. Alissa did a rough hop, a set of incomplete turns, and a fairly graceful leap. Then she and the boy began marching around the floor with the other pairs.

"She didn't tell me she had a partner," I mumbled to myself.

"Did you say something?" Aimee asked.

"Uh, no. It's nothing," I said quickly.

I had to be more careful. If I didn't watch out, my friends would realize that I was watching Alissa's routine much more closely than was necessary. I had decided not to tell them about the switch. I was still unsure about all this.

But I kept feeling like I was keeping something from them. What would be the harm in telling them? It did seem that involving the Forever Friends Club helped in solving big problems. That's what friends are for! Just look at all the problems Aimee had when she tried to keep Graham's reading problems from the group. Things worked out better for everyone, even Graham, when she finally told us what was going on.

But I wasn't ready to tell them just yet. I wanted to make sure I could even dance Alissa's part before I made a full confession. Then I knew I would need their help.

"Hey, do you want to explore the theater?" Krissy suggested after we had watched the rehearsal for an hour. "I've never been in one of these places, except when it was full of people and I couldn't look at anything."

"I want to go back outside and look at the fountains and the other buildings of Lincoln Center," Aimee said.

"Don't they have the opera in one place and the symphony in the other?" Linda Jean asked.

"I think so," said Aimee.

"Yes, let's go," I said. I wanted to take a look backstage and find all the entrances and exits. Besides dancing Alissa's part for her, I had to figure out a way to switch places with her without anyone seeing us.

"Take a break!" the director yelled.

"Joy, everyone, come up here," Alissa invited us onstage.

We all jogged up the steps to the stage. I looked out at the seats. The house lights were on, and we could see row upon row up to the top of the theater.

"How many people will be here tonight?" I asked, my voice cracking a little.

"The State Theater holds 2,500 people, more or less," answered the cute boy that Alissa had danced with. "Alissa tells me you are her friends from Atlanta, Georgia. I'm Russell."

"You were great up there," I said after introducing myself and the other girls. "Will you be at Alissa's birthday party tomorrow?"

"I wouldn't miss it. Alissa and I have been in dance class together since we were little kids."

"But Russell dances regularly with the ballet companies around town, and I try to avoid it," Alissa said.

"If you put your mind to it, you would be as great at ballet as you are at all the other things you do," Russell told her.

"Russell is 14. So, he thinks he knows everything!" Alissa scoffed and then laughed.

He's 14, I thought. No wonder he was so good. He had plenty of years of classes and practice.

"Do you want me to teach you the steps to the dance?" our hostess asked casually.

"Count me out," Linda Jean said, backing away. "I'm going to go talk to the light people."

Aimee and Krissy made excuses and wandered off also. *Perfect*, I thought. So, during the break, it was just Alissa and me onstage, learning the steps to her dance. When we were almost through, Russell came back onstage to tell us it was almost time for rehearsal to start again.

"You're very good, too," he complimented me. "I was watching you from backstage. Do you want me to run through it once with you?"

"Sure she does," Alissa said, pushing me forward. "Just pretend you're me," she added in a whisper to me.

Back at Alissa's house that afternoon, I floated around in the imaginary arms of Russell, pretending we were Clara and the Prince instead of a couple of toy soldiers. Every spare minute, I practiced the steps to the dance.

Krissy had to keep asking me to pay attention to the preparations for the party.

"Here, hang these streamers," she said. "Can you believe how big this room is? I'm beginning to wonder if we'll ever transform it into a circus tent."

Most of the houses we had decorated took less than an hour. We had already been working diligently for three hours, and only half of the room was done.

Mrs. O'Toole sailed into the room. "What a splendid job you're doing!" she gushed. "Do you need any help finishing anything?" she asked us sweetly.

After she had left the room again, I whispered to Linda Jean, "It's weird how she's always so nice to us, and with Alissa, she's so strict about everything."

"As far as I can tell, nothing about the O'Toole family is ordinary," Linda Jean said.

"Listen, speaking of unusual things, I need to talk to all of you about the ballet tonight," I said suddenly.

Everyone turned and looked at me expectantly.

"I'm going to dance Alissa's part instead of her dancing it," I blurted out. "I need you to help us make the switch. I figured we could all go up to the dressing room to wish her good luck before the performance, and then Alissa and I could change clothes..."

"Are you nuts? You'll never pull it off," Aimee said.

"Yes we will. I've been practicing all day, and I even did the dance once with Russell. Come on, Forever Friends. Alissa needs me. And what's more important is that she needs us."

Ten

"**I** can't believe I'm really doing this," I said as we entered the theater.

Abby looked at me strangely. "What are you doing, Joy?"

I coughed. "Uh, seeing the ballet in New York, of course. It's a dream come true."

She smiled. "Well, calm down. You're a bundle of nerves. Anyone would think it was you who's performing instead of Alissa."

My stomach did a somersault. It was a good thing Abby wasn't looking back at the wide eyes of the Forever Friends behind her. Their surprised looks would have given me away for sure.

The usher showed us to our row of seats. *And, of course, they turned out to be excellent seats*, I thought sarcastically. They weren't as good as front row center, but they certainly were close enough for everyone to comfortably watch the performance. Suddenly, I wished that I could sit down and just relax to the beautiful music and dancing that soon would be filling the theater.

"Before we get settled, let's go backstage and wish Alissa good luck," Linda Jean said perfectly on cue.

This was the cue we had arranged to get us all backstage for the switch.

"I'm sure Alissa will appreciate that," Abby told us. "I'll wait here, though, if you don't mind."

"Oh, we don't mind at all, Abby," Krissy said quickly.

"And by the way, Joy," she called after us.

I stopped, barely able to breathe. I didn't turn around because I was sure she'd be able to read the fear on my face.

"Your new hat is very becoming on you," Abby replied.

"Thanks, Abby," I said and continued walking. "Whew, that was close," I whispered after we got backstage. "Thank goodness you didn't make her any more suspicious with that comment about staying there," I said to Krissy as we went around to the stage door entrance.

"Me?" shrieked Krissy. "What about you and your bundle of nerves?"

"Okay, so she guessed the truth. But she doesn't know it's really the truth. She thinks she was just teasing me."

At the stage door, we gave our names, and the man stepped aside to let us pass.

"So far so good," I said.

Alissa was waiting in the women's chorus dressing room on the fourth floor. The men's chorus was one floor below, and the principal dancers and soloists dressed on the second floor. The first floor, of course, was the stage.

"Thanks for coming by," Alissa said loudly in the corridor before pulling us into the room. "Are you ready? We have about five minutes before the rest of the dancers come in to get changed," Alissa told me.

In no time at all, Alissa had painted my cheeks red and had my hair combed exactly like hers with my bangs over my eyes. Alissa dressed in my clothes with my new hat pulled down over her face.

"Now, don't worry," Alissa said. "I won't speak to your mother or my mother. And you don't have to talk to anyone here because I hardly know them."

"What about Russell?" I asked nervously.

"Pretend you just came down with laryngitis and can't talk," Alissa suggested.

"This scheme will probably blow up in all our faces," I said.

"No, it won't," Alissa said. "You're going to be fantastic." She lifted the brim of my hat and peered out at my eyes, which were peeking out from under my bangs. "You're the best friend I've ever had," she said softly. "The absolute best."

The lights blinked once and then twice.

"We'd better go if we're going to see the show. Break a leg," Linda Jean told me.

"Break two," Aimee said, giving me the thumbs-up sign.

Krissy hugged me quickly.

Then crowds of dancers pushed their way into the dressing room for final makeup and hair checks. They didn't pay any attention to me. The loudspeaker piped the orchestra's opening song into the dressing room. I couldn't believe it. I was really there. I was a ballet dancer for real!

"You're looking good tonight, Alissa," one of the other cast members said as she sat next to me at the mirror.

I only nodded, pointing to my throat.

"Laryngitis, huh?" she asked sympathetically. "At least it doesn't affect your feet."

I managed a smile. If only I could be me for just a moment. I'd love to meet the fellow members of the cast. Most of all, I'd love to know that Abby knew she was watching me, her daughter, dancing on the New York stage.

The music started. My mouth was dry, and my palms were wet. The narrator made the introduction, telling the audience the story of Clara and the enchanted world she enters when her godfather gives her a nutcracker doll. Then before I knew it, the cue was given for the children to skip into the room to open presents.

"This is it," I murmured. I could feel the dinner I had eaten doing flip flops in my stomach. This was more than just normal stage fright. This was sheer terror.

"But, I'm going to do it," I kept telling myself. "I'm going to do this for Alissa—and for me."

The strains of soft music faded and then crashed as the godfather entered dressed all in black and glittery stars. Clara acted surprised, and then it was time for the soldiers to put on their hats.

I reached for my hat. It slipped from my fingers, and I had an instant picture in my head of thousands of people laughing at me.

Russell handed my hat to me with a smile. "Relax," he said.

I took five deep breaths and let them out slowly as we walked into position. I told myself to just pretend I was home in Atlanta, on the Community Hall stage, performing *Sleeping Beauty*. I had to think of anything but those 2,500 people watching me. *I am Alissa O'Toole, famous actress of stage and screen, and now, famous ballerina,* I thought.

The march began.

"That's our cue," Russell said, gently taking my arm. "Smile, Alissa. I know you're going to be terrific."

I was nervous. I was scared. But I was ready.

From my first ballet-slippered step, I was a different person. Whenever I go onstage, I become the music. I become a part of the dance.

My pointed toes were perfect, and my box step was flawless. Russell and I did our dance in perfect unison, sliding and leaping together. My hours of practice earlier that day had paid off. I knew Alissa's dance as well as if I had been rehearsing it for months.

Even when I felt the heat of the spotlight centered directly on Russell and me, I didn't waver. I lifted my gun onto my shoulder and did three leaps in a row, and then I joined Russell in the line with the other soldiers.

All too quickly, the lights went off, and the curtain was lowered.

"You were great!" Russell exclaimed as we exited the stage. "I've never seen you so together. You did our turns beautifully. Come on, Alissa. How come you've never danced that well before? You've been holding out on me."

At that moment reality came crashing back. I didn't even thank Russell for his praise, even though my heart was singing.

"I have to go," I whispered.

"But, Alissa...wait!" he yelled.

I raced off toward the dressing room, hoping Russell wouldn't follow me. "It's too bad," I told Alissa a moment later as we exchanged clothes and I scrubbed off my makeup. "I would like to get to know Russell better. He seems like a nice guy."

"Who knows?" she replied. "Maybe you'll get your chance at the party tomorrow."

"Right," I said. "The party. I still haven't figured out a dance for the party."

"Tell your mom the bathrooms were really crowded," she told me before I ran out.

"Why?" I asked her.

"Because that's where I said I was going during intermission."

I pulled my hat down over my eyes and charged off down the corridor.

"I'll see you later, Alissa," Russell said as I breezed past him in the hall.

I lifted up the brim of my hat. "Sorry. It's me, Joy," I said.

He scrunched his eyebrows in a puzzled frown. "I'm sorry, Joy," he said. "For a minute there, you looked just like Alissa."

"Well, I'll see you at the party tomorrow!" I called over my shoulder. I had to get out of there before he suspected just how close he was to discovering our secret.

* * * * * * * *

All anyone thought about the next day was the party. I finally found some time to choreograph a simple dance. Linda Jean fussed with her experiments, and Aimee made origami

116

circus animals until there were elephants, horses, lions, and tigers hanging all over the room.

Patty was so excited when Alissa invited her to the party. Patty even came early to help out. In fact, she ended up greeting guests at the door and doing name tag duty because I was still practicing my dance.

"Welcome, everyone," Mrs. O'Toole said when all the guests had assembled in the game room. "We were waiting for Alissa's father to arrive before we started, but it looks as though the airport is backed up. So, we'll go ahead and begin."

She motioned Alissa up onto the stage area that we had set up. As usual, Alissa was her formal self, not at all like the fun Alissa who had taken us all over the city.

"I wish there was something we could do to make her act like a kid for her own party," I said to Aimee.

"How about sending her mother out of the room?" Aimee asked hopefully.

"I think she's more disappointed that her dad isn't here than anything else," Patty said, leaning close to me. "Remember how sad she sounded when she told us that he was away all the time on business?"

"That's right," said Linda Jean. "And she told us at dinner the other night that her father had missed her last two birthday parties."

"Well, we'll just have to make this party the best one ever. Maybe she'll loosen up and enjoy herself," I said hopefully. "Hey, there goes Krissy."

Krissy went up to the stage and began her act. By the time she was done with the card tricks, Alissa was chuckling. In the middle of Krissy's act, the rest of us couldn't help but overhear Abby and Mrs. O'Toole talking. They were standing on the other side of the curtain and couldn't see us.

"I know Alissa acts differently around me than she does around you and the girls," Mrs. O'Toole told Abby. "For some reason, she thinks I want her to act like an adult all the time."

"Have you given her any reason to feel that way?" we heard Abby ask.

"We shouldn't be listening to their conversation," Aimee whispered.

"Shhh!" I told her. "It might help Alissa to know what her mother says."

Mrs. O'Toole cleared her throat. "Having an actress for a daughter isn't the easiest thing. It seems as if I have to make decisions for her constantly. I try to protect her and direct her career at the same time."

"It must be a difficult job," Abby sympathized.

"It's especially difficult since my husband is rarely around," Mrs. O'Toole explained.

"We have the same situation at our house," Abby told her. "My husband is gone all week, so Joy and I are on our own."

"We really shouldn't be listening," Aimee said again.

"Shhh!" I replied.

"Joy seems so well adjusted," Mrs. O'Toole observed.

I couldn't help smiling at that.

"Joy and I make decisions together," Abby said. "We're partners more than we are mother and daughter. Whenever possible, I want Joy to learn to make her own choices. Perhaps you and Alissa could do the same thing. It's pretty hard to shoulder all the responsibility yourself."

"We definitely should not be eavesdropping," I said, suddenly not wanting to hear anything else about Abby and me.

"Shhh!" said Aimee, Patty, and Linda Jean at the same time.

"But what if Alissa decides not to do a show or take classes that I know would be good for her career?" Mrs. O'Toole asked.

Abby was quiet for a moment. Finally, she said, "Would there be any harm in Alissa's slowing down for a while, even if she misses a few movies or TV shows? She's still very young, and there will be many opportunities for her in the future."

We sneaked away as Mrs. O'Toole agreed with Abby's last comment.

"And now it's time for the disappearing box trick," Krissy announced.

I stepped forward from behind the curtain to assist.

"You'll notice that this is just an ordinary cabinet," Krissy said, waving her magician's wand toward the refrigerator box that we had fixed up for the occasion.

Krissy turned the box around, being careful not to let the curtain show the opening in the back of the cabinet. First, we'll use Joy as our victim, ahem, I mean assistant."

I stepped into the box and quickly slid

through the opening and out behind the curtain.

Out front, Krissy was opening the front curtain to show the audience that I had disappeared.

"And now, to bring her back." She tapped on the box three times and said, "Piggle, wiggle, niggle, smush."

Just as I was climbing back into the box, someone tapped me on the shoulder.

"I'm Mr. O'Toole," the man whispered. "Do you think I'd fit in there?"

"Just a second," I cautioned him.

Krissy opened the front curtain on the box. Obviously, I wasn't there. "Oh, Joy? Joy, where are you?" She stuck her head in the box and looked around.

"Do it again," I whispered from behind the curtain.

"We'll try this one more time," Krissy said to the laughing audience. "This time, all of you have to say the magic words with me."

Together, the famous actors and actresses, dancers, and singers crowded into Alissa's game room to say the magic words.

When Krissy pulled the curtain back dramatically, the crowd gasped. Out of the box stepped Mr. O'Toole.

Alissa ran up onstage and hugged her father. "If nothing else happens, this is the best birthday ever!" she exclaimed.

"On with the show," Aimee said. She stepped forward and gathered the guests into groups for craft time.

As I went over to help Aimee, I saw Alissa sitting between her father and mother. To my surprise, they were all laughing over trying to copy Aimee's origami animal-folding techniques.

Then Linda Jean showed off her crazy scientific experiments, and Aimee wowed them all with her songs. Finally, it was time for me to perform.

"May I have some music, please? And feel free, anyone, to join in the dance after I've shown you the steps," I announced.

The steps to my dance were simple, and the beat of the music was contagious. Soon the others, including Alissa and her parents, were up and dancing to the rhythm of the music.

When the music wound down, Alissa said, "Do something else, Joy. You dance so well. How about a little ballet?"

"I'm sorry," I said. "I don't have the right

kind of music with me."

"I have something," Russell said, pulling a tape from his pocket. "You can improvise."

The music of the toy soldier march from last night's ballet filled the room. Startled, I looked at Russell and then at Alissa.

"Dance with her, Russell," Alissa said.

Then, looking at me, Alissa said, "It's time I told my parents the truth."

Russell came and stood next to me. I quickly took my position. Soon I was part of the music, in tune with the dance.

"You knew all along that it was me onstage with you instead of Alissa," I accused as Russell danced next to me, just as he had done so perfectly the night before.

"I didn't know at first. But you moved more elegantly than Alissa had in practice. And Alissa talks a lot. I knew something was up when she, I mean you, didn't say a word," Russell said as we marched in a square.

"Oh?" I did two quick leaps past him.

I smiled and marched off the stage to the rousing applause of the birthday guests.

I looked up, and Alissa's parents were smiling, too. I guessed that Abby's talk with Mrs. O'Toole was helpful.

"I can't thank you enough for the party you have given my daughter," Mr. O'Toole said to us later when we were all having refreshments.

We all watched Alissa blow out her candles after we sang "Happy Birthday" to her.

While the other guests were busy talking to each other, Alissa's mom made her way over to where the Forever Friends and Patty were talking to Alissa.

Looking at Alissa and then at the other Forever Friends, Mrs. O'Toole said, "I have been pushing Alissa a bit too hard lately. The lengths she went to just to get out of dancing in the ballet boggles my mind. I think our family needs to sit down and start planning together. We haven't had a good talk in a long time."

"Doing Alissa's birthday party has been fun," I told her. "I think Alissa is terrific."

"It was much more than you say, Joy," Mrs. O'Toole insisted. "Sometimes it takes strangers to come in and make you see what has been under your nose all along."

We looked away as she exchanged a warm look with Abby.

"I hope we've become friends," Abby said to her.

"Oh, well, that, too," she said, waving her hand. She didn't want anyone to see the tears in her eyes. "I want to pay you extra for all the work you've done, and for saving Alissa's reputation at the ballet."

"Thanks, Mrs. O'Toole, but I think I speak for all of us when I say that just being here in New York is enough payment," I said.

The other members of Party Time gathered around me nodding their heads.

"We've had a fabulous vacation, shopped in the most famous stores in the world, and had such a blast!" Aimee added.

"We can't put a price on our friendship with Alissa. We don't want you to pay us for having such a great time and for making a new friend," I said. "The trip here has been more than enough."

Even the big ball dropping on Times Square on New Year's eve the following night couldn't be as exciting as what happened next.

Alissa joined the group and stood next to Patty. "What I've really missed by taking all the classes and being in all the films and shows is having a real friend," Alissa said. "I'd love to be a member of the Forever Friends Club. Could I?" she asked us.

"Of course, you can," we all said. There was a lot of hugging and crying, and we all promised to write to each other often.

"You know," Alissa said, pulling Patty closer to her. "Patty and I could start the New York City chapter of the Forever Friends Club. Maybe we could even do parties. What do you think, Patty?"

"Count me in," she said with a big grin. "I'm a pretty good cook. And I could teach kids how to make stuff."

"I could dance and sing. And we could both play games," Alissa added.

"What about me?" Russell asked. "I couldn't help but overhear your conversation. Can I join the Forever Friends Club, too? I'm sure I could learn a few magic tricks."

"We'd need a lot of help from Party Time in Atlanta, though," Patty said. "I mean, couldn't you put together a party kit with recipes and suggestions for party themes to get us started?" she asked with bubbling enthusiasm.

I smiled at all of my friends. "Sure! That's what friends are for," I answered. Then I added, "Hey, Forever Friends, we could be onto the start of something big!"

About the Author

CINDY SAVAGE lives in a big rambling house on a tiny farm in northern California with her husband, Greg, and her four children, Linda, Laura, Brian, and Kevin.

She published her first poem in a local newspaper when she was six years old, and soon after got hooked on reading and writing. After college she taught bilingual Spanish/English preschool, then took a break to have her own children. Now she stays home with her kids and writes books for children and young adults.

In her spare time, she plays with her family, reads, does needlework, bakes bread, and tends the garden.

Traveling has always been one of her favorite hobbies. As a child she crossed the United States many times with her parents, visiting Canada and Mexico along the way. Now she takes shorter trips to the ocean and the mountains to get recharged. She gets her inspiration to write from the places she visits and the people she meets along the way.